OWN iT! 1

WORKBOOK
WITH EBOOK
Lynn Durrant

CAMBRIDGE
UNIVERSITY PRESS

Shaftesbury Road, Cambridge CB2 8EA, United Kingdom

One Liberty Plaza, 20th Floor, New York, NY 10006, USA

477 Williamstown Road, Port Melbourne, VIC 3207, Australia

314–321, 3rd Floor, Plot 3, Splendor Forum, Jasola District Centre, New Delhi – 110025, India

103 Penang Road, #05–06/07, Visioncrest Commercial, Singapore 238467

José Abascal, 56–1°, 28003 Madrid, Spain

Cambridge University Press & Assessment is a department of the University of Cambridge.

We share the University's mission to contribute to society through the pursuit of education, learning and research at the highest international levels of excellence.

www.cambridge.org
Information on this title: www.cambridge.org/9781009043519

First published 2020

20 19

Printed in the Netherlands by Wilco BV

A catalogue record for this publication is available from the British Library

ISBN 978-1-009-04351-9 Own it Workbook with eBook Level 1
ISBN 978-8-490-36069-9 Collaborate Workbook Level 1

Additional resources for this publication at www.cambridge.org/ownit/resources

Cambridge University Press & Assessment has no responsibility for the persistence or accuracy of URLs for external or third-party internet websites referred to in this publication and does not guarantee that any content on such websites is, or will remain, accurate or appropriate. Information regarding prices, travel timetables, and other factual information given in this work is correct at the time of first printing but Cambridge University Press & Assessment does not guarantee the accuracy of such information thereafter.

CONTENTS

VOCABULARY AND READING
Months, cardinal and ordinal numbers and colours

1 ⭐ **Complete the sentences with the months in the box and ordinal numbers.**

> April   August   February   ~~January~~
> June   March   November   October

1 ___January___ is the first month.

2 _____ is the _____ month.

3 _____ is the third month.

4 _____ is the _____ month.

5 May is the _____ month.

6 _____ is the sixth month.

7 July is the _____ month.

8 _____ is the _____ month.

9 September is the _____ month.

10 _____ is the tenth month.

11 _____ is the _____ month.

12 December is the _____ month.

2 ⭐⭐ **Complete the crossword. Write seven more colours.**

ACROSS →

2 three letters

3 four letters

4 six letters

7 five letters

8 five letters

DOWN ↓

1 five letters

5 six letters

6 four letters

```
    ¹G
   ²R _ _
³_ _ _ E
    E   ⁵_   ⁶_
⁴_ _ _ N _
         ⁷_ _ _ _
⁸_ _ _ _ _ _
```

Online profile

3 ⭐⭐ **Read about Dasha and Carlos. Where are their friends from?**

Home	**Profile**	Photos	Events

INTERNATIONAL STUDENT PROFILE DAY!

Hello! My name's Dasha. I'm from Warsaw in Poland. I'm 11. How old are you? In this photo, I'm with my two best friends. Polina is Polish, but Marta isn't Polish. She's Brazilian. My favourite colour is green. What's your favourite colour? My birthday is on 10th April. When's your birthday? My dream is to be a doctor! What's your dream? Write soon!

Hi, Dasha! I'm Carlos and I'm 11, too! I'm Mexican, from Mexico City. In this photo, I'm with my best friends. They're not Mexican. Yusuf is from Turkey and David is from England. My favourite colour is blue. I'm 12 tomorrow! It's 5th June and it's my birthday! My dream is to be a singer! Who's your favourite singer?

Let me know! 😊

4 **Read the profiles again and complete the table.**

Name	Birthday	Favourite colour	Dream
Dasha	10th April	green	⁴_____
¹ Carlos	²_____	³_____	singer

5 ⭐⭐ **Circle the correct answers.**

1 Dasha is from *China* / (*Poland*).

2 Her birthday is in the *fourth* / *seventh* month of the year.

3 Carlos is from *Turkey* / *Mexico*.

4 His birthday is in the *sixth* / *twelfth* month of the year.

5 *David* / *Carlos* is 12 tomorrow.

LANGUAGE IN ACTION AND VOCABULARY

Subject pronouns and possessive adjectives

1 ⭐ **Complete the table with the subject pronouns in the box.**

> it   they   we   ~~you~~

Singular	Plural
I	³ _____
¹ _you_	you
he / she / ² _____	⁴ _____

2 ⭐ **Write the subject pronoun.**

1 Dasha _____ she _____
2 photos _____
3 school _____
4 Carlos _____
5 Polina and Marta _____
6 Yusuf and I _____

3 ⭐ **Which plural pronoun can we use for objects and people?**

_____

4 ⭐ **Complete the sentences with the possessive adjectives in the box.**

> her   his   its   my   our   ~~their~~   your

1 Yusuf and Carlos are at school. They're in _____ their _____ classroom.
2 He's from Poland. _____ name's Max.
3 I'm 12 years old and _____ best friend, Alba, is 11.
4 We're from China. _____ nationality is Chinese.
5 You're 13. _____ birthday is in April.
6 My teacher is Maria. _____ birthday is in August.
7 This school is nice. _____ classrooms are big!

Verb *be*

5 ⭐⭐ **Complete the profile with the correct form of *be*.**

My name ¹ _____ is _____ Sofía.
I ² _____ from Chile. My best friend ³ _____ Ana. She ⁴ _____ (not) from Chile. She ⁵ _____ from Brazil. My favourite singer ⁶ _____ Lorde. My favourite songs ⁷ _____ *Green Light* and *Royals*. They ⁸ _____ brilliant!

Question words

6 ⭐ **Match questions 1–5 with answers a–e.**

1 Where are you from?   [c]
2 How old are you?   ☐
3 When's your birthday?   ☐
4 Who's your best friend?   ☐
5 What's your favourite number?   ☐

a 10th May.   d That's Alba.
b It's 15.   e I'm 11.
c ~~I'm from Paris.~~

Classroom objects

7 ⭐ **Look at the pictures. (Circle) the correct words.**

1 It's a *board* / (*calculator*).   4 They're *pens* / *pencils*.
2 They're *chairs* / *desks*.   5 It's a *pen* / *pencil*.
3 It's a *window* / *door*.   6 They're *rulers* / *notebooks*.

LISTENING AND LANGUAGE IN ACTION

A talk

🎧 **1** ⭐ Listen and (circle) the correct answer.
S.01

Elena's from *Spain / Brazil*.

🎧 **2** ⭐ Listen again. Number the instructions in the order you hear them (1–4).
S.01

🎧 **3** ⭐⭐ Listen again. Are the sentences *T* (true) or *F* (false)?
S.01

1 This is Elena's first day at school.   T

2 She's from the capital of Brazil. _____

3 She's the only student from Brazil in her class. _____

4 Her notebook is on her desk. _____

5 Her pens and pencils are in her schoolbag. _____

6 The ruler on the desk is hers. _____

Whose + possessive pronouns

4 ⭐⭐ Complete the sentences with the correct possessive pronouns.

1 Whose dictionaries are these?
They're their dictionaries. They're _____theirs_____ .

2 Whose ruler is this?
It's my ruler. It's _____ .

3 Whose books are these?
They're our books. They're _____ .

4 Whose poster is that?
It's her poster. It's _____ .

5 Whose chairs are those? They're your chairs.
They're _____ .

6 Whose calculator is this? It's his calculator.
It's _____ .

Imperatives

5 ⭐⭐ Put the words in the correct order to make sentences.

1 write / Don't / notebook / my / in
Don't write in my notebook.

2 board / the / Write / the / words / on
_____

3 late / Don't / for / be / class
_____

4 teacher / to / Listen / the
_____

5 eat / in / class / Don't
_____

6 book / your / Close
_____

6 ⭐⭐⭐ Write two more instructions for your class.

_____

_____

_____

_____

WRITING
An informal letter

1 ⭐ Read Jenny's letter. Who is from Australia?

20 Marsh Street
York
Yorkshire
DN14 68YK

20th October

Dear Lucy,

1 My name is Jenny Watts and I'm 12. I'm from York in England.

2 My school is great. The classroom is green, orange and white. It's very nice, with lots of posters on the walls. Our teacher is friendly and I'm happy in my new class.

3 My best friend isn't in my class. She's at a different school. She isn't English like me, she's Australian. Her name is Sarah.

4 My favourite object is my new red and blue notebook. My favourite number is five – my birthday is 5th May! My dream is to be a famous singer.

All the best,

Jenny

2 ⭐ Read the letter again. Match topics a–d with paragraphs 1–4.

a favourite object, number, birthday and dream ☐

b name, age and nationality ☐1

c best friend ☐

d school and class ☐

3 ⭐ Match phrases 1–3 with functions a–c.

1 All the best, ☐

2 Our teacher is friendly <u>and</u> I'm happy in my new class. ☐

3 Dear Lucy, ☐

a to start a letter

b to end a letter

c to join two ideas in one sentence

Write an informal letter.

PLAN

4 ⭐⭐ Decide what information to include in each paragraph. Use the information in Exercise 2 to help you.

WRITE

5 ⭐⭐⭐ Write your letter. Remember to include four paragraphs, the address and date, and expressions from the *Useful language* box (see Student's Book, p9).

CHECK

6 Do you …

• introduce yourself and give your name, age and nationality?

• use *and* to join ideas?

• say what your dream is?

1 FRIENDS AND FAMILY

 Carlos Maria

Marta David Javier   Lucía

Lucas Ana (Me!)   Pedro Julia

VOCABULARY
Family members

1 ⭐ Find 13 more words for family in the word search.

W	G	N	E	P	H	E	W	G	S	O	N
B	R	O	T	H	E	R	D	F	T	S	E
R	A	D	G	U	J	I	N	K	M	O	X
A	N	U	T	S	S	K	J	I	E	A	Y
V	D	W	H	B	C	U	N	C	L	E	D
G	M	U	M	A	K	E	H	K	M	Y	A
D	A	T	S	N	H	D	A	D	W	D	U
G	R	A	N	D	A	D	E	Q	I	F	G
R	G	U	W	J	O	P	R	T	F	Q	H
B	D	N	I	E	C	E	I	M	E	P	T
F	G	T	K	H	O	S	N	G	X	V	E
C	O	U	S	I	N	S	I	S	T	E	R

2 ⭐ Match 1–8 with a–h to make family word pairs.

1 brother   [f]   a mum
2 nephew   [ ]   b wife
3 husband   [ ]   c daughter
4 grandad   [ ]   d aunt
5 uncle   [ ]   e grandma
6 dad   [ ]   f ~~sister~~
7 son   [ ]   g granddaughter
8 grandson   [ ]   h niece

3 ⭐ Which family word in Exercise 1 can be male or female? _____

4 ⭐⭐ Look at Ana's family tree. Complete her sentences with the correct family words.

1 Carlos is my ___grandad___ and María is my
_____ .

2 Marta is my _____ and David is my
_____ .

3 Javier is my _____ and Lucía is my
_____ .

4 Lucas is my _____ .

5 Pedro and Julia are my _____ .

5 ⭐⭐ (Circle) the correct answer.

> **DAVID**   Hi! I'm David and my sisters are April, May and June. This is my mum.
>
> **MUM**   Hi! I'm a mum with four children. My daughters are April, May and June and this is my son. His name is _____ .

a July   b September   c David

Explore it!

Guess the correct answer.

_____ is the most popular boy's name in the UK in the last 500 years.

a Robert   b John   c James

Find another interesting fact about names. Then send a question in an email to a classmate or ask them it in the next class.

READING

A webpage

1 ⭐ Read the webpage. What is it about? (Circle) the correct title.

a A big family
b A small family
c A family from Canada

2 ⭐⭐ Read the webpage again and underline the words. Then check their meaning and complete the sentences.

> dentist   everyone   fun
> ~~neighbours~~   whole

1 Your house is next to mine. We're _neighbours_ .
2 My aunt is a _____ . Her job is to look at teeth!
3 A _____ day is 24 hours long.
4 My favourite day is Sunday with friends and family. It's _____ !
5 This lesson is for all students. It's for _____ .

3 ⭐⭐ Read the webpage again. Are the sentences *T* (true) or *F* (false)?

1 Tom is English.   ___T___
2 His mum is a teacher.   _____
3 His family is typical because it's big.   _____
4 His cousins are in a different street.   _____
5 The family are together in the morning and evening.   _____
6 Tom is happy at home.   _____

4 ⭐⭐ (Circle) the options that are true for you.

1 My family is *big* / *small*.
2 My favourite time of day is the *morning* / *evening*.
3 My neighbours *are* / *aren't* at my birthday parties.

Tom is from Durham in England. He's seven years old today! His parents' names are Helen and Richard. His mum is a dentist and his dad is a teacher at a secondary school.

Tom's family isn't very typical. He's got two brothers and three sisters, and his grandma and grandad are at home with them, too. Tom's aunt, uncle and four cousins have got a house in front of his. The whole family are in the same street!

Tom's favourite times are the morning and the evening. That's when his family are all together for breakfast and dinner – there are ten people around the table!

Birthdays in Tom's family are fun, too. They've got a birthday party every month! Today, everyone is at Tom's party: his family, his friends and his neighbours.

Is Tom happy in his big family? Yes, he's got good friends at school, and lots of brothers, sisters and cousins at home!

LANGUAGE IN ACTION

have got: affirmative and negative

1 ⭐ (Circle) the correct options.

1 Richard and Helen (*have*) / *has* got six children.

2 My grandma *have* / *has* got a red car.

3 I *haven't* / *hasn't* got a big family.

4 My dad *haven't* / *hasn't* got any cousins.

5 My friend's parents *have* / *has* got a big house.

6 Uncle David *haven't* / *hasn't* got any children.

2 ⭐⭐ Complete the text with the correct form of *have got*.

My name is Claudia. I'm from Mexico but I live in Australia with my family. I ¹ *'ve got* a big family. I ² _____ five brothers and two sisters. My parents ³ _____ a big house – it's perfect for a big family! My dad's name is Javier. He ⁴ _____ lots of brothers and sisters, too. My mum is called Sandra. She ⁵ _____ a brother in Mexico – that's my Uncle Sergio. I ⁶ _____ any aunts or uncles in Australia. They're all in different countries. My best friend, Helen, is Australian. She ⁷ _____ any brothers or sisters, it's only her! She ⁸ _____ a small family, but they're good fun! 🙂

3 ⭐⭐ Write the words in the correct order to make sentences. Then match them with pictures a–e.

1 bike / I / haven't / a / got

I haven't got a bike. _____ b

2 My / got / grandad / hasn't / a / mobile phone

_____ ☐

3 home! / We've / pets / at / four / got

_____ ☐

4 best friends / at / school / two / I've / got

_____ ☐

5 My / two / got / boards / classroom's

_____ ☐

Possessive *'s*

4 ⭐⭐ Complete the sentences with the possessive *'s* and a family word.

1 My mum *'s mum* is my grandma.

2 My cousin_____ is my uncle.

3 My dad_____ is my uncle.

4 My mum_____ is my aunt.

5 My brother_____ is my mum.

6 My dad_____ is my grandad.

5 ⭐⭐⭐ Find four facts about a famous family. Write four sentences about them. Use the correct form of *have got* and the possessive *'s*.

Victoria and David Beckham have got four children.

_____

_____

_____

_____

VOCABULARY AND LISTENING
Describing people

1 ⭐ **Complete the list with the words in the box.**

blonde   freckles   ~~grey~~   tall   wavy

Describing people

Eyes: ¹ _grey_ , brown

Hairstyle: long, short, ² _____

Hair colour: ³ _____ , brown, grey, red

Height: ⁴ _____ , short

Other features: beard, ⁵ _____ , glasses, moustache

2 ⭐ **Match the descriptions (1–4) with the photos (a–d).**

1 glasses and long wavy hair

2 long hair and a beard

3 long blonde hair

4 short brown hair and glasses

A conversation

🎧 3 1.01 ⭐⭐ **Listen to the students talking about their families. Write** *Paul's family*, *Emma's family*, *Jon's family* **or** *Sue's family* **under the correct pictures.**

🎧 4 1.01 ⭐⭐ **Listen again.** Circle **the correct answers.**

1 Paul's got four / *five* brothers and sisters.

2 Paul *has* / *hasn't* got blonde hair.

3 Emma's sister *has* / *hasn't* got freckles.

4 Emma's got a friend with *long* / *short* hair.

5 Jon's got *one brother* / *two brothers*.

6 Jon's mum *is* / *isn't* short.

7 Sue's got *one tall brother* / *two tall brothers*.

8 *Sue's* / *Tony's* hair is red.

5 ⭐⭐⭐ **Describe a friend. Include information from each category in Exercise 1.**

My friend's name is Cindy. She's got brown eyes and long red hair.

_____

_____

_____

LANGUAGE IN ACTION
have got: questions

1 ⭐ Complete the table with *have*, *has*, *hasn't* or *haven't*.

¹ _____Have_____ you got any cousins?	Yes, I ²_____.	No, I ³_____.
⁴_____ they got red hair?	Yes, they ⁵_____.	No, they ⁶_____.
⁷_____ she got green eyes?	Yes, she ⁸_____.	No, she ⁹_____.
How many sisters ¹⁰_____ he got?	He ¹¹_____ got two sisters.	

2 ⭐ Complete the questions with the correct form of *have got*. Then match them with answers a–f.

1 _____Have_____ you _____got_____ any brothers and sisters? ☐b a No, he hasn't.
2 _____ your niece _____ brown hair? ☐ b ~~No, I haven't.~~
3 _____ you and your family _____ a big house? ☐ c Yes, they have.
4 _____ your dad _____ a beard? ☐ d Yes, she has.
5 _____ your parents _____ a car? ☐ e Yes, it has.
6 _____ your house _____ a lot of rooms? ☐ f No, we haven't.

3 ⭐⭐ Complete the conversation with the correct form of *have got* and the words in brackets.

BETH Hi, Jan. ¹*Have you got* (you) a lot of homework?

JAN No, I ²_____.

BETH Good. I've got some questions for a school project. ³_____ (you) any brothers and sisters?

JAN Yes, I ⁴_____. I've got two brothers. They're twins.

BETH ⁵_____ (they) green eyes like you?

JAN Yes, they ⁶_____!

BETH Cool! And ⁷_____ (your mum) brown hair like you?

JAN No, she ⁸_____. She's got blonde hair.

4 ⭐⭐⭐ Read the answers from an interview with a famous actor. Write questions with *have got*. Use *how many* when necessary.

1 *Have you got a big house?*
   Yes, I have. My house is very big.
2 _____ ?
   Yes, we've got five children, including twins!
3 _____ ?
   We've got three boys and two girls.
4 _____ ?
   My wife's got a horse, and the children have got two rabbits.
5 _____ ?
   Yes, I have. I've got two Oscars!

WRITING
An informal email

1 ⭐ **Look at the photos and read the email. Which photo is of Kylie and Kate? Tick (✓) the correct photo.**

● ● ●

TO: Ed

FROM: Kate

Hi Ed,

1 How are things? I'm in a new school and I've got a new friend. This email is about her.

2 I ¹'m / 've got a lot of friends in my class, but one girl ²'s / 've my best friend. Her name ³'re / 's Kylie. We say we ⁴'re / 've twins – we look the same! We ⁵'s / 've got brown hair and green eyes, and we ⁶'re / 've got the same birthday! It ⁷'s / 're funny! 😆 And we ⁸'s / 've both got a little brother. My brother ⁹'re / 's ten and Kylie's brother ¹⁰'s / 're nine.

3 The photo is of Kylie and me at basketball. Kylie's good fun and a great friend. 🙂

4 Have you got good friends at your new school? Have you got a best friend? Email me soon!

That's all for now,

Kate

2 ⭐⭐ (Circle) **the correct contractions in the email.**

3 ⭐⭐ **Read the email again. Are the sentences *T* (true) or *F* (false)?**

1 Kate and Kylie are best friends. _____T_____

2 They are in different classes. _____

3 Their birthdays are on the same day. _____

4 Kate hasn't got brown hair. _____

5 Kylie hasn't got green eyes. _____

6 They have both got a little brother. _____

7 Kate's brother is ten. _____

4 ⭐⭐ **Match topics a–d with paragraphs 1–4 in the email.**

a extra information about a photo   ③

b description of a new friend at school   ☐

c introduction and reason for writing   ☐

d Kate's questions for Ed   ☐

Write an informal email to a friend about a new school friend.

PLAN

5 ⭐⭐ **Make notes about these things:**

your friend's name and age

_____

your friend's physical description and family

6 **Decide what information to include in each paragraph. Use the information in Exercise 4 to help you.**

WRITE

7 ⭐⭐⭐ **Remember to include four paragraphs, the verbs *be* and *have got* and expressions from the *Useful language* box (see Student's Book, p17).**

CHECK

8 **Do you …**

• use expressions to start and end your email?

• give information about your friend in the second paragraph?

• use information from a photo in the third paragraph?

• ask questions in the last paragraph?

VOCABULARY

1 Look at the family tree. Are the sentences *T* (true) or *F* (false)? Correct the false sentences.

1 Ashley is Kyle's cousin.

_____

2 Jane is Mary's daughter.

_____

3 Jon is Ashley's grandad.

_____

4 Luke is Andrea's cousin.

_____

5 Jane is Kyle's mum.

_____

6 Luke is Jane's brother.

_____

7 Kyle and Harry are Jon's grandsons.

_____

8 Ashley is Rob's aunt.

_____

9 Rob is Ashley and Kyle's dad.

_____

10 Holly and Ashley are Mary's nieces.

_____

2 Circle the odd one out.

1 moustache / beard / tall   4 blue / green / short

2 wavy / glasses / short   5 long / blonde / red

3 blonde / freckles / brown   6 brown / tall / wavy

LANGUAGE IN ACTION

3 Circle the correct options.

Victor and Anna ¹*has / have* got a big house. It ²*'s / 've* got a big garden and seven rooms. They ³*'s / 've* got one daughter called Siena. They ⁴*haven't / have* got any sons. Anna and Siena ⁵*has / have* got blonde hair. Anna ⁶*'s / 've* got blue eyes, and Siena ⁷*'s / 've* got brown eyes. Victor ⁸*'s / 've* got three sports cars. They're his favourite! Anna ⁹*hasn't / haven't* got a sports car, but she ¹⁰*'s / 've* got a mobile home!

4 Write questions with the correct form of *have got*. Use *how many* when necessary.
Then look at Exercise 3 and answer the questions.

1 Victor and Anna / a big garden?

_____   _____

2 rooms / their house?

_____   _____

3 they / sons?

_____   _____

4 Siena / blonde hair?

_____   _____

5 sports cars / Victor?

_____   _____

6 Anna / mobile home?

_____   _____

CUMULATIVE LANGUAGE

5 Match questions 1–8 with answers a–h.

1 Have your grandparents got a big garden? ☐
2 What have we got for homework? ☐
3 How many cousins have you got? ☐
4 Have you got an English dictionary? ☐
5 Has your dad got a beard? ☐
6 When have we got our exam? ☐
7 Is that Amalia's baby brother? ☐
8 Wow! How many books have your parents got? ☐

a I've got four.
b Yes, they have. It's my favourite place!
c I don't know. I think they've got hundreds!
d No, he hasn't! But he's got a moustache.
e Yes, I have.
f We've got the exercises on page 14.
g No! It's her nephew. He's her sister's baby.
h I'm not sure. I think it's in November.

2 THAT'S LIFE!

VOCABULARY
Daily routines

1 ⭐ **Complete the crossword. Use the clues.**

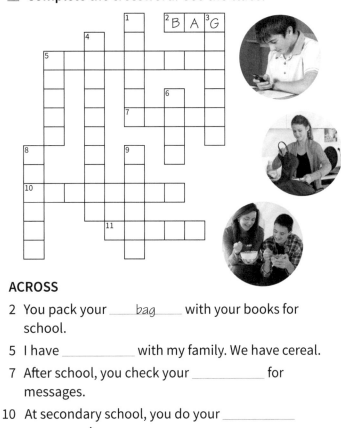

ACROSS

2 You pack your ___bag___ with your books for school.

5 I have _____ with my family. We have cereal.

7 After school, you check your _____ for messages.

10 At secondary school, you do your _____ every evening.

11 First you wake up. Then you _____ .

DOWN

1 I _____ at seven o'clock, but I get up at 7.15.

3 At night, you _____ and sleep.

4 In the morning, I _____ in my school uniform.

5 I _____ my teeth after breakfast and before I go to bed.

6 After school, I go _____ on the bus.

8 I go to _____ from Monday to Friday, but not at the weekend!

9 I have a _____ when I get up and after sport.

2 ⭐ **Complete the daily routines with the verbs in the box.**

| brush   check   do   get (x2) |
| go (x3)   have (x2)   pack   wake |

1 _get_ up   7 _____ to school

2 _____ dressed   8 _____ my phone

3 _____ my teeth   9 _____ to bed

4 _____ breakfast   10 _____ up

5 _____ home   11 _____ a shower

6 _____ my bag   12 _____ my homework

3 ⭐⭐ **Complete the text with the correct form of the phrases from Exercise 2.**

This is my ideal school day. I ¹ ___wake up___ at nine o'clock and I ² _____ for messages. I ³ _____ at 9.15, I have a shower and I ⁴ _____ in my favourite clothes. Then I ⁵ _____ (cereal). At ten o'clock, I brush my teeth, I ⁶ _____ with my books, and I ⁷ _____ on the bus. I have three classes and I go home to have lunch. I haven't got any homework! After dinner, I check my phone again and ⁸ _____ .

4 ⭐⭐⭐ **Write about your ideal school day. Use Exercise 3 to help you.**

This is my ideal school day. I …

_____

_____

_____

Explore it! 🖱️

Guess the correct answer.

People in the UK *get dressed / have a shower* in eight minutes.

Find an interesting fact about daily routines in your country. Then send a question in an email to a classmate or ask them it in the next class.

READING
A profile

1 ⭐ **Read the profile. Is this sentence _T_ (true) or _F_ (false)?**

Dylan has got 25 hours of classes a week. _____

A day in the life of a
child actor

Dylan Roberts is 14, and he's a child actor. He makes films and doesn't go to school. He always has classes with special teachers called film tutors. Child actors usually have 15 hours of classes a week (schools have 25), but it isn't easy! Dylan often has lots of work to do.

2 ⭐⭐ **Read the profile again and <u>underline</u> these words. Then check their meaning in a dictionary and complete the sentences.**

> break   busy   filming
> ~~make-up~~   tutor

1 Here's the green ___make-up___ for your eyes.
2 After three classes, we've got a _____ to have lunch.
3 All the actors are ready for _____ today.
4 I've got a _____ for extra English classes.
5 Our weekends are very _____ with lots of things to do!

3 ⭐⭐ **Read the profile again. (Circle) the correct answer.**

1 Dylan is a child actor. He _goes_ / (_doesn't go_) to school.
2 Dylan's special teacher is a film _tutor_ / _actor_.
3 A child actor _has_ / _hasn't_ got a lot of work to do.
4 Dylan has breakfast at _home_ / _work_.
5 Dylan's first classes are _before_ / _after_ filming.
6 He hasn't got any _homework_ / _breaks_.

4 ⭐⭐ **What's your opinion? Read the statements and write _Yes_ or _No_.**

1 It's easy to be a child actor. _____
2 Fifteen hours of classes a week is a good idea. _____
3 Dylan's day is fun. _____
4 Not having homework is great. _____

Dylan talks about his typical day:

'I get up at six in the morning and get dressed. At 6.15, a car takes me to filming. I have breakfast at work and then I practise the day's filming for an hour. At 8.00, they do my hair and make-up and I get dressed in my film clothes. Filming starts at 9.00. Then, at 11.00, I have a break for half an hour. After that, I go to the tutor's room for classes. I don't have any homework. At 6.00 in the evening, I go home or to a hotel. I have a shower, have dinner, read my part of the film for tomorrow, and go to bed. It's a busy day!'

LANGUAGE IN ACTION

Present simple: affirmative and negative

1 ⭐ (Circle) the correct options.

1 Dylan is a child actor and he *make* / (*makes*) films.
2 Child actors *don't* / *doesn't* live at home when they are in a film.
3 They *eat* / *eats* dinner in a hotel.
4 We *study* / *studies* English.
5 Martha *have* / *has* breakfast at school.
6 Film tutors *teach* / *teaches* small classes.

2 ⭐ Write the third person singular of the present simple.

have	watch	meet	go
1 has	2	3	4

play	brush	do	hurry
5	6	7	8

3 ⭐⭐ Complete the text with the present simple form of the verbs in brackets.

● ● ●

Veera is 12. She ¹ _goes_ (go) to school in Finland, and her class ² _____ (have got) 18 students. School ³ _____ (start) at 9.45 am and it ⁴ _____ (finish) at 2.45 pm. There are three or four classes a day. In Finland, students ⁵ _____ (not have got) homework or exams. Veera ⁶ _____ (have got) a lot of free time. After school, she ⁷ _____ (meet) her friends and they ⁸ _____ (go) to a sports club for lunch. Veera ⁹ _____ (love) sport and she ¹⁰ _____ (play) in the school football team. Her dream is to be a footballer!

Adverbs of frequency

4 ⭐ Match the adverbs of frequency with the ticks (✓) and cross (✗).

1 always [c]   a ✓ ✓
2 usually [ ]   b ✗
3 often [ ]   c ✓ ✓ ✓ ✓
4 sometimes [ ]   d ✓
5 never [ ]   e ✓ ✓ ✓

5 ⭐ Are these statements true for you? Write *T* (true) or *F* (false).

1 I often do my homework with my friends. _____
2 I always check my phone when I wake up. _____
3 My best friend sometimes has lunch at my house. _____
4 I never go to bed late at the weekend. _____
5 I usually have lunch with my grandparents on Sundays. _____

6 ⭐⭐ Write the words in the correct order to make sentences.

1 makes / dad / often / dinner / My
   My dad often makes dinner.
2 I / brush / after / teeth / always / my / breakfast
   _____
3 go / at / They / lunchtime / usually / home
   _____
4 sometimes / We / class / are / for / late
   _____
5 I / check / in / never / my / class / phone
   _____
6 does / in / the / Dan / park / homework / his / usually
   _____

VOCABULARY AND LISTENING
Leisure activities

1 ⭐ **Complete the leisure activity phrases.**

1 play an ins _trum_ ent
2 go for a b_____ e r_____ e
3 read a book or a ma_____ e
4 chat on_____ e
5 play v_____ o g_____ s
6 make v_____ s
7 take ph_____ s
8 download s_____ s
9 listen to m_____ c
10 go sh_____ g
11 hang out with fr_____ s
12 watch _____ V

2 ⭐⭐ **Complete the sentences with the correct form of the phrases from Exercise 1.**

1 Lucy often ____ _downloads songs_ ____ from the internet – she doesn't buy CDs.

2 When I _____ with my friends, we talk for hours on our computers or phones.

3 I usually meet and _____ in the park after school.

4 Luke's sister plays the guitar, but he doesn't _____ .

5 I use my phone to _____ – my friends are the actors. I sometimes put them on *YouTube*!

6 They never _____ now, they always find films and series online.

Street interviews

🎧 **3** ⭐ **Listen to the interviews.** (Circle) **the correct answer.**
2.01

The interviews are about different …

a school activities.
b hobbies.
c instruments.

🎧 **4** ⭐⭐ **Listen again and number the activities in the photos in the order you hear them (1–3).**
2.01

🎧 **5** ⭐⭐ **Listen again and write *A* (Anja), *C* (Callum) or *D* (Debra).**
2.01

1 __A__ does his/her hobby every day.
2 _____ and _____ do their hobbies at the weekend.
3 _____ does his/her hobby early in the morning.
4 _____ does his/her hobby with animals.
5 _____ uses the internet for his/her hobby.
6 _____ wants to do his/her hobby as a job.

6 ⭐⭐⭐ **Write about one of your hobbies. Use the questions below to help you.**

Where?   How often?   When?   Who with?

_____
_____
_____
_____
_____

LANGUAGE IN ACTION
Present simple: questions

1 ⭐ **Complete the questions with *Do* or *Does*. Then match them with answers a–f.**

1 _Do_ you see your friends at the weekend? ☐ b
2 _____ your parents like the same music? ☐
3 _____ your sister watch TV a lot? ☐
4 _____ your cousin hang out with you? ☐
5 _____ all your family play an instrument? ☐
6 _____ this timetable have ten subjects? ☐

a No, they don't.
b ~~Yes, I do.~~
c Yes, he does.
d Yes, we do.
e No, she doesn't.
f Yes, it does.

2 ⭐⭐ **Write the words in the correct order to make questions. Use the photos to help you.**

1 friends / you / online / Do / your / chat / with / ?
   Do you chat online with your friends?

2 download / your / Does / best friend / songs / ?
   _____

3 go / for / Do / you / Sundays / a / bike / ride / on / ?
   _____

4 shopping / Do / you / go / a lot / ?
   _____

5 play / games / your / dad / video / Does / ?
   _____

6 your / books / Does / read / mum / ?
   _____

3 ⭐⭐ **Answer the questions in Exercise 2 for you. Use short answers.**

1 _____   4 _____
2 _____   5 _____
3 _____   6 _____

Wh- **questions**

4 ⭐ **Circle the correct question words.**

1 (What) / When do you do at the weekend?
2 Where / Who do you go after school?
3 What / Who does Emir have lunch with?
4 Where / What do you usually meet Ada?
5 How often / Who do they go shopping?
6 Where / What time do you wake up on Mondays?

5 ⭐⭐ **Complete the interview with a tennis player. Write questions using the words in brackets.**

JADE	What time ¹ _do you get up_ (you / get up), Alina?
ALINA	Very early! At seven o'clock.
JADE	² _____ (you / get up) early at weekends, too?
ALINA	No, not always.
JADE	And how often ³ _____ (you / hang out) with friends?
ALINA	I see my friends twice a week.
JADE	⁴ _____ (your friends / come) to your matches?
ALINA	Yes, sometimes they do.
JADE	Great! And ⁵ _____ (your parents / watch) you, too?
ALINA	Yes. My dad comes to all my matches.
JADE	Nice! And ⁶ _____ (other people / ask) you to do interviews?
ALINA	No, they don't! I'm not famous!

WRITING
An article

1 ⭐ **Read the article.** (Circle) **the correct title.**

a What does Zev do at the weekend?

b What is Zev's daily routine?

Zev's from the USA. He's 12 years old. In his free time, he's a photographer. Zev's photos are of animals and objects. He often makes photo stories. He uses digital technology and his imagination.

1 This is a typical day in Zev's life. He always gets up at 7.00 and has a shower. At 7.30, he has breakfast. At 7.45, he brushes his teeth and packs his bag. He then goes to school at 8.00.

2 In the afternoon, Zev goes home. At 3.00, he usually has lunch and does his homework. He goes for a walk with his sister at 5.00 and looks for ideas for his photo stories.

3 From 6.30 to 8.00 in the evening, Zev makes his photo stories and puts them on his website. He sometimes chats online with his friends, but he never stays late. At 9.30, Zev goes to bed.

One day, I want to take photos like Zev!

2 Match topics a–c with paragraphs 1–3.

a description of Zev's evening routine ☐

b description of his morning routine ☐

c description of his afternoon routine ☐

3 ⭐ **Read the article again. What time does Zev do these things?**

1 gets up ___7.00___

2 has breakfast _____

3 packs his bag _____

4 goes to school _____

5 has lunch _____

6 goes for a walk _____

7 makes his photo stories _____

8 goes to bed _____

4 ⭐ **Find and <u>underline</u> five adverbs of frequency in the article.**

5 ⭐⭐ **Rewrite the sentences with the correct punctuation.**

1 how does Zev make his photo stories

*How does Zev make his photo stories?*_____

2 zevs sister doesnt take photos

_____

3 zevs friends look at his photo stories on his website

_____

4 wow I think the photos are great

_____

Write an article about someone's day.

PLAN

6 ⭐⭐ **Choose a person with a different daily routine from yours. It can be a friend or someone from your family. Decide what information to include in each paragraph. Use the information in Exercise 2 to help you.**

WRITE

7 ⭐⭐⭐ **Write your article. Remember to include the information in the correct order, the present simple, adverbs of frequency and correct punctuation from the *Useful language* box (see Student's Book, p29).**

CHECK

8 Do you …

- include an interesting title with a question?
- introduce the person, their nationality and what they do?
- describe the person's morning, afternoon and evening routines?
- end the article with a sentence about you and your ambition?

VOCABULARY

1 Complete the text with the words in the box.

> brush do dressed get go (x2)
> have pack shower up

I wake ¹_____ at 6.30 and I
²_____ up at 7.00. Then I have a
³_____ and ⁴_____ my teeth.
I get ⁵_____ in my school clothes and
⁶_____ my bag for school. At 7.30, I
⁷_____ breakfast with my mum and dad. I
⁸_____ to school at 8.30 and finish at 3.30.
In the afternoon, I ⁹_____ my homework
and then I've got some free time. In the evening,
I have dinner with my parents and then I
¹⁰_____ to bed at about 10.00.

2 Match the verbs with the activities.

1	chat	☐	a songs
2	download	☐	b a bike ride
3	go for	☐	c online
4	listen to	☐	d a book or a magazine
5	hang out with	☐	e music
6	read	☐	f friends
7	go	☐	g TV
8	watch	☐	h shopping

LANGUAGE IN ACTION

3 Complete the sentences with the present simple form of the verbs in brackets.

1 I _____ (not wake up) early at the weekend.

2 Martin _____ (go) to school at 9.00 every day.

3 We _____ (not do) our homework at school.

4 Tom's dad _____ (make) videos of his birthday every year.

5 Isabela _____ (not have) a big breakfast, only fruit.

6 Theo _____ (not play) the guitar very often.

4 Circle the correct option.

1 Daniel _____ shopping with his mum.
   a sometimes goes   b goes sometimes

2 I _____ video games with my brother.
   a play often   b often play

3 My dad _____ to rock music!
   a listens never   b never listens

4 We _____ with friends at weekends.
   a always hang out   b hang out always

5 They finish their homework and they _____ TV.
   a watch often   b often watch

5 Complete the questions and answers with the present simple form of the verbs in brackets. Add *Wh-* question words where necessary.

1 A: _____ you _____ (brush) your teeth every day?   B: Yes, I _____.

2 A: _____ your mum _____ (pack) your bag for you?   B: No, she _____.

3 A: _____ your cousins _____ (play) an instrument?   B: No, they _____.

4 A: _____ time _____ Chris _____ (go) home?   B: At 7.00.

5 A: _____ often _____ you _____ (read) a book?   B: Every month.

6 A: _____ _____ you _____ (go) on Sundays?   B: I often go to the park with my family.

CUMULATIVE LANGUAGE

6 Complete the conversation with the missing words. (Circle) the correct options.

ROSA   ¹_____ do you do in your free time?

MIRA   I ²_____ my best friend or go with my brother for a bike ride.

ROSA   ³_____ you see your best friend every day?

MIRA   Yes, most days. ⁴_____'s your best friend?

ROSA   That's Susan, but I ⁵_____ her all the time.

MIRA   ⁶_____ often do you see her?

ROSA   It depends, but usually every weekend. We sometimes ⁷_____ basketball on Saturdays.

MIRA   Hey! I play, too. What ⁸_____ do you meet on Saturdays?

ROSA   Usually in the afternoon.

MIRA   ⁹_____ to hang out one Saturday?

ROSA   Sure! ¹⁰_____ your phone? Here's my number.

MIRA   Yes, I ¹¹_____. OK, great!

1 a What   b Where

2 a meet usually   b usually meet

3 a Does   b Do

4 a Who   b When

5 a don't see   b doesn't see

6 a When   b How

7 a play   b plays

8 a often   b time

9 a You want   b Do you want

10 a Have got you   b Have you got

11 a have   b have got

SCHOOL DAYS

VOCABULARY
School subjects

1 ⭐ **Complete the subjects with the correct letters.**

1 Eng⌐ish
2 Spani__h
3 desig__ __nd techn__logy
4 m__ths
5 musi__
6 ar__
7 d__ama
8 geo__raphy
9 histor__
10 foo__ technology
11 P__
12 sci__nce
13 I__T

2 ⭐ **Write the correct school subjects from Exercise 1.**

1 _____music_____

2 _____

3 _____

4 _____

5 _____

6 _____

7 _____

8 _____

3 ★★ **Write the subjects for the definitions.**

1 You learn to play an instrument. _____music_____
2 You learn a language that people speak in lots of countries in South America. _____
3 You learn about people, countries and places. _____
4 You learn about things in the past. _____
5 You learn about numbers, shapes and space. _____
6 You learn a language that people speak in the UK and the USA. _____
7 You learn about food and what is good or bad to eat. _____
8 You do experiments. _____

4 ★★ **Write the names of these subjects in your language. Write S if they are similar to the words in English or D if they are different.**

1 science _____ _____
2 geography _____ _____
3 drama _____ _____
4 art _____ _____

Explore it! 🖱

Guess the correct answer.

One school in Lucknow, India, has got a lot of students. How many students has it got?

a about 15,000   b about 27,000   c about 52,000

Find an interesting fact about school subjects in another country. Then send a question in an email to a classmate or ask them it in the next class.

READING

A webpage

1 ⭐ **Read the webpage about schools in Singapore. Why don't teachers like posters in maths classrooms?**

| HOME | STORIES | PHOTOS |

SCHOOLS IN SINGAPORE

STUDENTS FROM SINGAPORE OFTEN GET VERY GOOD MARKS FOR MATHS AND SCIENCE IN INTERNATIONAL TESTS.

In maths lessons, students can use technology to answer the different maths problems. Their answers go on the whiteboard at the front of the class. All students can see and talk about their classmates' answers.

A lot of maths classrooms don't have posters on the walls. Teachers don't think posters help students learn.

Students can't talk to each other a lot. They work alone, but they can ask the teacher questions when they don't understand something.

In science classes, students can work on their projects once a week. In one class, they can build a robotic arm and in another class students can make a small radio.

In many secondary schools in Singapore, students don't do a lot of drama, language, music or art. Some teachers say, 'Art subjects aren't very important. Students need to be good at science and maths. They need these subjects for their adult life'. Is this a good or a bad idea? What do you think?

2 ⭐⭐ **Read the webpage again and <u>underline</u> these words. Then check their meaning in a dictionary and complete the sentences.**

> ~~adult~~   alone   build
> marks   whiteboard

1 In many countries, you're an _____adult_____ when you're 18.
2 My teacher always writes the answers on the _____ .
3 I never get good _____ in geography. Maps are difficult!
4 We want to _____ a robot for our project.
5 **A:** Do you need help?
   B: No, thanks. I always do my homework _____ .

3 ⭐⭐ **Answer the questions.**

1 What subjects are students from Singapore often good at?
   _____maths and science_____
2 What do teachers show on the whiteboard?
   _____
3 How do students work in maths classes?
   _____
4 How often do students work on science projects?
   _____
5 Which subjects are not very important in many schools?
   _____

4 ⭐⭐⭐ **Answer the questions with your own ideas.**

1 'Art subjects aren't very important.' What do you think?
   _____
2 Which subjects do you think are important? Why?
   _____

LANGUAGE IN ACTION
can for ability and permission

1 ⭐ (Circle) the options that are true for you.

1 In our classes, we *can / can't* put posters on the walls.

2 At break time, we *can / can't* play and talk to friends.

3 We *can / can't* talk in science classes.

4 We *can / can't* build interesting things for our projects.

5 Sometimes we *can / can't* work in groups in our English classes.

2 ⭐⭐ Complete the sentences. Use *can/can't* and the verbs in brackets.

1 My dad ___can't sing___ because he hasn't got a good voice, but he _____ amazing pictures. (sing / draw)

2 My cousin _____ good photos but she _____ videos. She's really bad at it! (take / make)

3 My mum _____ salsa quite well and she _____ the guitar, too. She's really good at it! (dance / play)

4 My little brother's four. He _____ English very well but he _____ it. (speak / read)

3 ⭐⭐ Complete the texts with *can/can't* and the verbs in brackets.

My favourite subject is history. I like it because we ¹ ___can work___ (work) in groups – it's great when we ² _____ (do) projects together. But we work alone when we have an exam – we ³ _____ (talk). After the exam we usually have a break and we ⁴ _____ (hang out) with friends.

RAJ

4 ⭐⭐ Write questions and short answers with *can*.

1 students / check their phone / in class? (✗)

   Can students check their phone in class?

   No, they can't.

2 students / ask questions / in class? (✓)

   _____

   _____

3 Kate / play the piano? (✓)

   _____

   _____

4 María / speak two languages? (✗)

   _____

   _____

5 students / work in groups / in maths classes? (✓)

   _____

   _____

6 you / do ballet? (✗)

   _____

   _____

5 ⭐⭐ Are these statements true for you? Write *T* (true) or *F* (false).

1 I can speak two languages. _____

2 I can dance salsa. _____

3 I can ride a bike. _____

4 I can play the guitar. _____

5 I can sing. _____

My favourite teacher is Mark, our geography teacher. I like his classes because we ⁵ _____ (ask) questions when we need to. We have options, too: sometimes we ⁶ _____ (choose) our homework and we ⁷ _____ (bring) interesting things to class. But we ⁸ _____ (be) late – Mark doesn't like that!

PAULA

VOCABULARY AND LISTENING

Places in a school

1 ⭐ **Read the definitions. Then (circle) the correct places in the spidergram.**

1 You can do outdoor sports here.
2 You can buy and eat food here.
3 You can do PE here.
4 Teachers can plan their lessons here.
5 You can leave your bag here.
6 You can read books and study here.
7 You can wash your hands here.

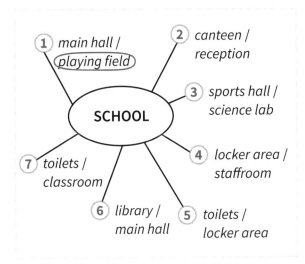

1 main hall / (playing field)
2 canteen / reception
3 sports hall / science lab
SCHOOL
4 locker area / staffroom
7 toilets / classroom
6 library / main hall
5 toilets / locker area

2 ⭐⭐ **Complete the text with places from Exercise 1.**

Mondays!

I don't like my timetable on Mondays! At 8.45 I go to ¹ ___reception___ and say hello to my aunt – she works at the school. Then I go to the ² _____ and put my sports shoes in my locker. After that, my class goes to the ³ _____ and we do experiments. I don't like science! At break time, I usually go to the ⁴ _____ for some food. Then we have PE in the ⁵ _____ and then lunch. In the afternoon, it's music and drama. At 4.15, we go to the ⁶ _____ and get a book to read – that's OK because I like books, but I'm always happy on Mondays at 4.30 because I can go home!

A radio programme

🎧 **3** 3.01 ⭐⭐ **Listen and number the places in the order you hear them (1–6).**

a □ main hall
b □ playing field
c □ canteen
d □ library
e 1 science lab
f □ music classroom

🎧 **4** 3.01 ⭐⭐ **Listen again. Are the sentences *T* (true) or *F* (false)?**

1 Alex likes the science lab. _____T_____
2 He likes the magazines from the library. _____
3 Alex's favourite subject is PE. _____
4 The music classroom is Alex's favourite place. _____
5 Marina has lunch in the canteen. _____
6 She likes all the places in the school. _____

LANGUAGE IN ACTION

Verb forms: (*don't*) *like, don't mind, love, hate* + *-ing*

1 ⭐ Match the verbs with the symbols.

1 love [b]   2 like [ ]   3 don't mind [ ]
4 don't like [ ]   5 hate [ ]

a 😕   b 😍   c 😠   d 😃   e 😐

2 ⭐⭐ Write sentences with the correct form of the verbs.

1 I / like / go / to the music club
   I like going to the music club.

2 We / hate / have / lots of homework
   _____

3 Tariq / not mind / do / sport in the sports hall
   _____

4 Gina / love / play / football / on the playing field
   _____

5 They / not like / learn / history
   _____

3 ⭐⭐ Complete the text with the correct form of the verbs in brackets.

I've got a twin brother but we're very different! He
¹ _hates getting up_ (hate / get up) early but I ² _____
(not mind / do) it for school. He ³ _____ (love / do) sport
and I ⁴ _____ (like / play) video games. I ⁵ _____
(not like / go) to parties. I ⁶ _____ (like / stay) at home.
My brother ⁷ _____ (love / hang out) with his friends
and ⁸ _____ (have) a good time.
He ⁹ _____ (not mind / study)
sometimes, but he doesn't love it.
I ¹⁰ _____ (love / learn) new
things, especially about science.

Object pronouns

4 ⭐ Complete the table with the object pronouns.

Subject	I	you	he	she	it	we	they
Object	¹ me	²	³	⁴	⁵	⁶	⁷

5 ⭐ Circle the correct option.

1 **A:** Do you like drama? **B:** Yes, I like (it) / them.

2 Mr Patel isn't at reception. Can you phone *her / him*?

3 I've got a problem. Can you help *me / it*, please?

4 Is Amaya here? I can't see *you / her*.

5 **A:** Do you like video games? **B:** I hate *it / them*.

6 What classes have we got today? Can you give *us / you* the timetable, please?

6 ⭐⭐ Look at the pictures and then complete the text with the correct subject or object pronouns.

Me (Josh)   **Lucas**

¡HOLA!

Lucas' mum   **Spanish**

I'm Josh, and Lucas is my best friend.
¹ _We_ (👦 + 👦) 're in the same
class and ² _____ (👦) lives near
³ _____ (👦). Lucas' mum is
Spanish. ⁴ _____ (👩) speaks
Spanish with ⁵ _____ (👦) at home,
but ⁶ _____ (👦) speak English with
⁷ _____ (👦 + 👩). We learn
Spanish at school and Lucas helps
⁸ _____ (👦) with my homework.
Spanish is difficult, but I like
⁹ _____ (¡HOLA!).

WRITING

A description

1 ⭐ **Read Sanjiv's description. Does he like his school?**

My school

1 *Courses and subjects*

I study at a very big school. Students can do different courses <u>such as</u> science or arts. I'm on the science course. I study English, maths and science and technology subjects, <u>like</u> computer science. That's my favourite subject.

2 _____

I really like the teachers. They teach regular classes, but they also teach some after-school clubs, <u>like</u> astronomy and dance. I like being with my teachers after class.

3 _____

We have six lessons a day and homework. I don't mind doing some homework, but I don't like a lot of it! I really like working with my classmates on group projects. I don't like working alone!

4 _____

Our school has got great places for lessons and activities. <u>For example</u>, we've got a big sports building, a canteen, an ICT room and three science labs. I love studying here.

2 ⭐ **Write the correct heading for each paragraph in the description.**

Great teachers ~~Courses and subjects~~

School places School routine

3 ⭐ **Read the description again. Then complete the text below with the phrases in the box.**

| computer science   doing a lot of homework |
| ~~the teachers at his school~~   working alone |

Sanjiv likes ¹ *the teachers at his school* and
² _____ . He doesn't like
³ _____ or
⁴ _____ .

4 ⭐ **Look at the <u>underlined</u> words and phrases in Sanjiv's description. What does he use them for? (Circle) the correct answer.**

a to join ideas

b to show different times

c to give examples

Write a description of your school.

PLAN

5 ⭐⭐ **Make a spidergram of your school in your notebook and use the plan below.**

6 **Decide what information to include in each paragraph. Use your spidergram and the information in Exercise 2 to help you.**

WRITE

7 ⭐⭐⭐ **Write your description. Remember to include four paragraphs, *can/can't* and expressions from the *Useful language* box (see Student's Book, p41).**

CHECK

8 **Do you …**

- give the name of the school in the opening sentence?
- include all of the information from your spidergram?
- give your opinion about studying at the school in your closing sentence?

VOCABULARY

1 Complete the school subjects.

1 Languages: E _ _ _ _ _ _ _ , S _ _ _ _ _ _ _
2 Numbers: m _ _ _ _
3 The past: h _ _ _ _ _ _
4 Countries: g _ _ _ _ _ _ _ _
5 In a lab: s _ _ _ _ _ _ _ , f _ _ _ t _ _ _ _ _ _ _ _ _
6 Art subjects: d _ _ _ _ _ and t _ _ _ _ _ _ _ _ _ ,
   d _ _ _ _ _ , m _ _ _ _ _ , a _ _
7 Sport: p _ _ _ _ _ _ _ e _ _ _ _ _ _ _ _
8 ICT: i _ _ _ _ _ _ _ _ _ _ and
   c _ _ _ _ _ _ _ _ _ _ _ _ _ t _ _ _ _ _ _ _

2 Find 12 places in a school in the word search.

R	O	L	O	C	K	E	R	A	R	E	A	N
E	P	I	C	O	M	E	C	H	I	B	J	S
C	A	B	S	T	A	F	F	R	O	O	M	P
E	N	R	E	R	I	H	A	L	F	K	J	O
P	L	A	Y	I	N	G	F	I	E	L	D	R
T	H	R	T	E	H	I	T	P	V	A	I	T
I	B	Y	O	C	A	N	T	E	E	N	C	S
O	C	E	I	H	L	A	C	T	E	R	T	H
N	O	S	L	E	L	O	R	R	N	E	R	A
S	C	I	E	N	C	E	L	A	B	Y	O	L
S	U	Y	T	T	H	I	P	R	M	E	O	L
C	L	A	S	S	R	O	O	M	O	P	M	S

LANGUAGE

3 Look at the table. Complete the sentences with *can/can't* and the correct verbs.

		OH YEAH!	¡HOLA!
Jon	✓	✗	✓
Lisa	✗	✓	✓

1 Jon _____ the guitar.
2 Lisa _____ the guitar.
3 _____ Jon _____ songs in English? _____ , he _____ .
4 _____ Lisa _____ songs in English? _____ , she _____ .
5 Jon and Lisa _____ Spanish.

4 Look at the symbols. Write sentences using (*don't*) *like, don't mind, love, hate* + *-ing*.

1 We / 😀 / talk to / our teachers _____

2 I / 😕 / do / homework _____

3 She / 😍 / listen / to music _____

4 They / 😕 / have / lunch at school _____

5 He / 😠 / be / late for class _____

5 Match questions 1–6 with answers a–f.

1 Does Tom like football? ☐

2 Does Berta play video games? ☐

3 Can you help Suzi? ☐

4 Is Harry in your class? ☐

5 Is this party for you and your friends? ☐

6 Do you like reading? ☐

a No, it isn't for us!

b No, he hates it!

c I don't mind it.

d Yes, she loves them.

e Yes, I can help her.

f Yes, he's with me.

CUMULATIVE LANGUAGE

6 Complete the conversation with the missing words. (Circle) the correct options.

DENIZ Hi, Kate! ¹_____ football today?

KATE No, I ²_____. It's Wednesday today.

DENIZ When ³_____ practice?

KATE On Tuesdays and Thursdays, and at the weekend ⁴_____ have matches.

DENIZ Oh! And ⁵_____ your parents watch your matches?

KATE It depends. ⁶_____ come and see me.

DENIZ Hey, ⁷_____ do we finish class today?

KATE At three o'clock! It's Wednesday, remember?

DENIZ Oh, great! Harry and I ⁸_____ for a bike ride after school on Wednesdays.

KATE ⁹_____ Harry now?

DENIZ He's in the library. He ¹⁰_____ a maths project to finish.

KATE Well, I love ¹¹_____. ¹² I go with you?

DENIZ Sure!

1 a Have you got   b You has got   c You have

2 a hasn't   b haven't got   c haven't

3 a do you have   b have you   c you have

4 a always we   b we always   c it always

5 a does   b do   c are

6 a They sometimes   b Them sometimes   c Sometimes them

7 a when   b who   c what

8 a go usually   b usually goes   c usually go

9 a What's   b Where's   c Who's

10 a 's got   b 've got   c haven't

11 a cycling   b cycle   c cycles

12 a Do   b Can   c Have

4 YOU ARE WHAT YOU EAT

VOCABULARY
Food and drink

1 ⭐ Complete the table with the words in the box.

> ~~apples~~ bananas beans cheese
> chicken eggs fish fizzy drink water

Food from plants	Food from animals	Drinks
apples		

2 ⭐⭐ (Circle) the correct answers in the quiz.

ALL ABOUT FOOD AND DRINK

1 Which food is NOT usually a cake?
   a chicken **b** chocolate

2 Which of these is NOT protein?
   a meat **b** carrots

3 Which of these is NOT from fruit?
   a juice **b** chocolate

4 Which of these is NOT from a plant?
   a meat **b** rice

3 ⭐⭐ Complete the food words in the text.

I'm Zara from Malaysia. I usually have kaya toast with [1]e_g_ _g_ _s_ for breakfast. I have lunch at school. Lunch is usually rice and [2]me_ _ or [3]ch_ _ _ _ _ _ curry with vegetables. I drink [4]ju_ _ _ made from orange and purple [5]ca_ _ _ _ _ _ and red [6]ap_ _ _ _ _. It's yummy! My mum cooks dinner. I love her [7]fi_ _ curry with [8]be_ _ _ _. We always drink [9]w_ _ _ _ .

4 ⭐⭐⭐ What is your favourite food for breakfast, lunch and dinner? Write about what you eat. Use Exercise 3 to help you.

I usually have …

_____

_____

_____

Explore it! 👆

Guess the correct answer.

Which country grows millions of bananas?

a the UK **b** Ecuador **c** China

Find an interesting fact about food in your country. Then send a question in an email to a classmate or ask them it in the next class.

READING

An article

1 ⭐ Read the article and match the foods in the box with the photos (1–3).

> blinis   herring with potatoes   mooncakes

Welcome to my festival!

1 _____

2 _____

3 _____

Hugo: Midsummer Eve, Sweden

I love this festival in June. It's at the start of the school holidays. We go to the countryside and in the morning we get some flowers for our hair. Then we dance to traditional music. Lunch is outside, and it's big! We always eat herring (a type of fish) with potatoes. Later, people play instruments and dance all night!

Mei Lin: Moon Festival, China

My favourite festival is in September, when we can see the first full moon of the month. We make paper lights and go to the park. And of course, we eat a mooncake or two! These are small round cakes (like the moon!) that have different fillings. I like the chocolate one. We give them to our friends and eat them together.

Daria: Maslenitsa Pancake Festival, Russia

This great festival is in February. We have fun activities for seven days! We do some sports, play music, dance and eat lots of food. I love having blinis. They are Russian pancakes made with butter, eggs and milk. We eat them with different toppings. My favourite topping is salmon and cream cheese. Yummy!

2 ⭐⭐ Read the article again and <u>underline</u> these words. Then check their meaning in a dictionary and complete the sentences.

> countryside   fillings
> full moon   pancakes   ~~toppings~~

1 What are your favourite _toppings_ on a pizza? I love extra cheese!

2 Once a month, we can see the _____ in the sky. It's completely round.

3 *Empanadas* are popular in South America. They have different _____ inside, such as meat or vegetables.

4 I love going to the _____ and looking at the trees and flowers.

5 We need milk and butter to make _____ .

3 ⭐⭐ Read the article again and complete the table.

Festival	Country	Month	Special food
Midsummer Eve	Sweden	1 June	2
Moon	3	4	mooncakes
Maslenitsa	5	February	6

4 ⭐⭐⭐ Answer the questions with your own ideas.

1 Which of the festivals is your favourite? Why?

_____

2 Think of a festival in your country. When is it? What food do you have?

_____

LANGUAGE IN ACTION
Countable and uncountable nouns

1 ⭐ **Write the correct headings in the table:** *Countable* or *Uncountable*.

1 _____	2 _____
cheese water bread _____*rice*_____ _____ _____	apple egg tomato _____ _____ _____

2 ⭐ **Complete the table in Exercise 1 with the words in the box.**

bean   carrot   chocolate   fish   ~~rice~~   taco

A/An, some/any

3 ⭐ Ⓒircle the correct options.

1 We use *a* or *an* with ⟨countable⟩ / *uncountable* nouns.

2 We use *some* and *any* with *singular* / *plural* countable nouns and uncountable nouns.

3 We use *some* in *affirmative* / *negative* sentences.

4 We use *any* in *affirmative* / *negative* sentences and questions.

4 ⭐⭐ **Complete the sentences with the words in the box.**

~~apple~~   chocolate   eggs   juice   sandwich

1 Have you got an _____*apple*_____ for your snack?

2 We haven't got any _____ for an omelette.

3 I'm hungry. Have you got a _____ for me?

4 Drink some _____ with your breakfast.

5 Can we have some _____ after dinner?

5 ⭐⭐ **Complete the conversation with *a, an, some,* or *any*.**

KIM What can we have for dinner? Have we got ¹_____*any*_____ rice?

DAN No, we haven't got ²_____ rice, but we've got ³_____ pasta.

KIM Pasta with cheese! Have we got ⁴_____ cheese?

DAN No. I can see ⁵_____ tomato and ⁶_____ egg, but that's all! Let's go to the shop.

KIM OK. Can you write a list? We need ⁷_____ cheese, ⁸_____ milk and ⁹_____ tomatoes. Is that all?

DAN No. We haven't got ¹⁰_____ drinks. We need ¹¹_____ juice.

KIM Right! And ¹²_____ chocolate!

6 ⭐⭐⭐ **What is your favourite dinner? What have you got at home to make it and what do you need? Write sentences with *a / an, some* and *any*.**

I want _____ for dinner.

I've got _____

I haven't got _____

I need _____

VOCABULARY AND LISTENING

Adjectives

1 ⭐ **Complete the adjectives with the missing vowels. Then match adjectives 1, 5, 7 and 10 with the photos (a–d).**

1 h o t [d]
2 d _ l _ c _ _ _ _ s
3 _ nh _ _ lthy
4 d _ sg _ st _ ng
5 sw _ _ t ▢
6 n _ c _
7 c _ ld ▢
8 h _ _ lthy
9 fr _ sh
10 s _ lty ▢

a

b

c

d

2 ⭐⭐ (Circle) **the correct options.**

1 Careful! The milk is *cold* / (*hot*)!
2 I don't like beans. They're *nice* / *disgusting*!
3 Ice cream is perfect for a hot day. It's *hot* / *cold* and *sweet* / *salty*.
4 Water is a *healthy* / *unhealthy* drink, but fizzy drinks are *healthy* / *unhealthy*.
5 I like having *disgusting* / *fresh* fruit for breakfast.

A quiz

🎧 3 ⭐ **Listen to the family. Do they answer all the questions in the quiz?**
4.01

_____

🎧 4 ⭐ **Listen again. Match the foods (1–3) with the restaurants (a–c).**
4.01

1

2

tacos

3

kebab

curry

a La Cantina   b Kumkapi   c Bangkok Garden

5 ⭐⭐ **Listen again. Are the sentences T (true) or F (false)?**

1 The restaurants in the quiz are new. ___T___
2 The names of the restaurants are in the first question. _____
3 The girl thinks Turkish food is sweet. _____
4 'Fresh' and 'healthy' describe two of the three types of food. _____
5 The boy thinks kebabs are delicious. _____
6 The children both want to go to the Mexican restaurant. _____

6 ⭐⭐⭐ **Do you prefer Mexican, Turkish or Thai food? Look on the internet for more information about these types of food. Write your ideas.**

I prefer _____ because it's _____

_____

_____

_____

LANGUAGE IN ACTION

there is/isn't, there are/aren't

1 ⭐ **Look at the picture of the restaurant. Circle the correct options.**

1 There *is* / *isn't* a picture on the wall.
2 There *is some* / *isn't any* water in the glasses.
3 There *is some* / *isn't any* food on the tables.
4 There *are some* / *aren't any* children.
5 There *are* / *aren't* eight people.
6 There *is* / *isn't* a window in the picture.

2 ⭐⭐ **Look at the picture and complete the questions and answers with the correct form of *there is* / *there are*.**

1 Is there_____ any juice?
  Yes_____, there is_____.
2 _____ any bananas?
  _____, there _____.
3 _____ any tomatoes?
  _____, there _____.
4 _____ any cheese?
  _____, there _____.
5 _____ any milk?
  _____, there _____.

much/many, a lot of

3 ⭐⭐ **Circle the correct options.**

My sister loves cooking and she's got ¹*a lot of* / *much* ideas for delicious meals. I like cooking, too, but I haven't got ²*many* / *much* time to help her. She often uses ³*a lot of* / *much* fruit and vegetables. She loves healthy food. Tonight, she wants to make pasta for dinner, but there isn't ⁴*many* / *much* pasta and there aren't ⁵*many* / *much* tomatoes in the fridge. The good thing is that there are ⁶*a lot of* / *much* restaurants near home!

4 ⭐⭐ **Complete the questions in the quiz with *much* or *many*. Then circle the correct answers.**

HOW MUCH DO YOU KNOW?

1 How _____ milk is there in 1kg of cheese?
  a two litres   **b** five litres
2 How _____ water is there in a banana?
  a 74%   **b** 90%
3 How _____ sugar is there in an average glass of orange juice?
  a about 21 g   **b** about 50 g
4 How _____ coffee beans are there in a 1kg bag of coffee?
  a about 1,500   **b** about 8,800

5 ⭐⭐⭐ **Look in your fridge and answer the questions.**

1 How much fruit is there?

_____

2 How many vegetables are there?

_____

WRITING
A description

1 ⭐ **Look at the menus and read the description. Which menu is from Eva's favourite place, a or b?**

My favourite place to eat
by Eva García

1 My name's Eva ¹(and) / but I'm from Chile. My favourite place to eat is a small café called Buenas Migas. I go there every Friday with my best friend and our parents.

2 Buenas Migas is near my house. There isn't a lot of space inside the café ²and / or it hasn't got many tables, ³or / but there are some more tables outside. We sit outside when the weather's nice.

3 You can eat different sandwiches, and they're all delicious! They've got egg, cheese, chicken ⁴but / or meat sandwiches and they're all healthy. My favourite is the egg sandwich.

4 To drink, you can have water, fizzy drinks ⁵but / or juice. Their orange and carrot juice is always fresh. It's definitely my favourite drink!

2 ⭐⭐ (Circle) **the correct options in the description.**

3 ⭐⭐ (Circle) **the correct options.**

We use ¹but / or when there is a choice (usually between two things).

We use ²but / and to contrast different information.

We use ³or / and to add similar information.

4 ⭐⭐ **Read the description again. Match topics a–d with paragraphs 1–4.**

a food (including your favourite) — ③

b introduction: who you are, what the description is about — ☐

c drinks (including your favourite) — ☐

d the place: where it is and what it is like — ☐

a Menu
Our sandwiches
egg
meat
cheese
vegetable
Our cold drinks
orange juice
water
fizzy drinks

b MENU
Our cold drinks
orange and carrot juice
water
fizzy drinks
Our sandwiches
meat
cheese
egg
chicken

Write a description of your favourite place to eat.

PLAN

5 ⭐⭐ **Make notes about your favourite place to eat. Say where it is, when you go there and what it is like. Decide what information to include in each paragraph. Use the information in Exercise 4 to help you.**

WRITE

6 ⭐⭐⭐ **Write your description. Remember to include four paragraphs, *there is/are*, countable and uncountable nouns and expressions from the *Useful language* box (see Student's Book, p53).**

CHECK

7 Do you …
- introduce yourself and say where you are from and the name of your favourite place?
- say what is your favourite type of food and drink?
- use adjectives to describe food?

VOCABULARY

1 Write the food or drink words. Use the picture to help you.

1 They are a vegetable. They are long and orange.

_ _ _ _ _ _ _

2 You can make cheese from this drink. _ _ _ _ _

3 It's usually brown and it's sweet. It's made from cacao. _ _ _ _ _ _ _ _ _ _ _

4 It's usually on top of pizzas. _ _ _ _ _ _ _

5 They come from chickens. _ _ _ _ _

6 It's a yellow fruit. There are lots in Ecuador.

_ _ _ _ _ _

7 You make this drink with fruit or vegetables.

_ _ _ _ _ _

8 It's a drink, but we also use it to have a shower.

_ _ _ _ _

2 Match the opposites.

1 healthy ☐   a disgusting
2 delicious ☐   b sweet
3 cold ☐   c unhealthy
4 salty ☐   d hot

LANGUAGE IN ACTION

3 Circle the correct option: *C* (countable) or *U* (uncountable).

1 apple   C / U
2 cheese   C / U
3 water   C / U
4 sandwich   C / U
5 bread   C / U
6 milk   C / U
7 potato   C / U
8 chocolate C / U
9 banana   C / U
10 bean   C / U

4 Complete the text with *a*, *some* or *any*.

It's my mum's birthday today and my dad and I want to make her a nice meal. We haven't got ¹_____ chicken, but we've got ²_____ meat to cook with ³_____ rice. There's ⁴_____ bottle of water in the fridge and we've got ⁵_____ fruit juice, too. There are ⁶_____ carrots and ⁷_____ tomatoes as well. We've got ⁸_____ book for my mum. She loves reading.

5 Complete the dialogue with the words and phrases in the box.

> Are there any   How many   Is there
> much   some   there are   There aren't

LUIS   Let's make dinner.

ANDREA OK. We can cook some chicken with vegetables. ¹_____ vegetables?

LUIS   Yes, ²_____. We've got three carrots and some tomatoes.

ANDREA ³_____ tomatoes are there? I need three.

LUIS   ⁴_____ three – only two.

ANDREA OK. ⁵_____ any cheese? We can have the tomatoes with some cheese.

LUIS   Yes, there's ⁶_____ cheese!

ANDREA Great. And how ⁷_____ chicken is there?

LUIS   A lot! We can eat chicken for dinner, breakfast and lunch!

CUMULATIVE LANGUAGE

6 Complete the conversation with the missing words. (Circle) the correct options.

VICTOR Mum, what ¹_____ for dinner?

MUM   There's ²_____ soup and fish. Do you want that?

VICTOR Yes, I'm hungry! And ³_____ can I have to drink?

MUM   ⁴_____ some fizzy water.

VICTOR Have we got any juice? I don't like ⁵_____ fizzy water.

MUM   Have a look in the fridge. I think there ⁶_____ two bottles of juice there.

VICTOR Yes! And it's orange juice – delicious! Do you want some juice, too?

MUM   No, thanks. I ⁷_____ like it much. I prefer water. ⁸_____ any apples for after your dinner?

VICTOR No, there ⁹_____ any, but there are some bananas. I ¹⁰_____ eat those.

MUM   You're hungry! There's ¹¹_____ food, and you can eat all of it!

VICTOR OK, Mum. Yes, I'm really hungry!

1 a there is	b is there	c are there
2 a some	b a	c an
3 a where	b what	c when
4 a There are	b There is	c There has
5 a drink	b drinking	c drinks
6 a are	b have	c is
7 a do	b don't	c 'm not
8 a Are there	b Is there	c Are they
9 a aren't	b isn't	c haven't
10 a am	b do	c can
11 a much	b a lot of	c many

5 WHAT'S YOUR STYLE?

VOCABULARY
Clothes

1 ⭐ Look at the photos and (circle) the correct words.

1 *boots /*
   (trainers)

2 *hoodie /*
   T-shirt

3 *jeans /*
   joggers

4 *boots /*
   flip-flops

5 *shorts /*
   skirt

6 *T-shirt /*
   jacket

2 ⭐ Look at the picture. Complete the text with the words in the box.

> boots cap jacket joggers
> shirt shorts trainers T-shirt

Laura's favourite outfit is a ¹___T-shirt___ ,
²_____, ³_____ and a
⁴_____. Alex's favourite outfit is a
⁵_____ and a ⁶_____,
⁷_____ and ⁸_____.

3 ⭐⭐⭐ What can you wear? Write at least three clothes items for each situation.

1 Your friends ask you to go to the mountains with them in December.

   I can wear _____

2 It's July and you have a picnic with your parents.

   _____

3 It's Saturday afternoon and you want to visit your grandma.

   _____

Explore it! 🖱

Guess the correct answer.

A *kurta* is a long shirt without a collar. Men and women from *South America / South Asia / Europe* wear kurtas.

kurta

Find an interesting fact about clothes in your country. Then send a question in an email to a classmate or ask them it in the next class.

READING

An online diary

1 ⭐ Read Marina's online diary. Who doesn't like purple?

_____

● ● ●

Marina'sFashionFriends.com

Sunday, 10.30 am

It's Sunday morning and I'm writing this post from the park. I'm here with my family. I can see a group of girls. They're talking and having some snacks. One girl looks great! I want her clothes! 😃 She's wearing purple jeans, an orange T-shirt, a black cap and some fabulous purple trainers. 👍 👟 I think those trainers are in a shop round the corner! Hmm … have I got the money to buy them?

14.00 pm (and back online!)

I'm at home and guess what? I've got those lovely trainers!

18.00 pm

Comments

Ethan: Hi, Marina! I always read your diary and I usually like your ideas. 😉 But sorry … I don't like purple. I think it's a horrible colour! 😖 It's a nice day today and I'm in a park, too. I'm wearing my new joggers and a T-shirt, but it's hot now and I'm not wearing my cap. What are you wearing?

Ada: Where can I buy those trainers? I want some, too. Ethan, purple is THE colour! I've got six purple T-shirts and a pair of purple shorts! I'm wearing my favourite purple T-shirt today!

20.00 pm

Ada, they're selling them in World of Trainers. I'm wearing them now!
Now I need some jeans. 👖
Sorry, Ethan, purple is THE colour! 😉

New post tomorrow!

2 ⭐⭐ Read the diary again and <u>underline</u> these words. Check their meaning in a dictionary and then complete the sentences.

> corner ~~fabulous~~ guess what
> lovely pair

1 I love my green boots. They're
_____fabulous_____!

2 _____? We're in the same class!

3 The clothes shop isn't far away. It's round the _____.

4 Sara's new skirt is _____. I want one!

5 You need to get a new _____ of shoes.

3 ⭐⭐ Read the diary again. Ⓒircle the correct answers.

1 It's Sunday and Marina *is /* (*isn't*) at home.

2 She likes *one girl's / some girls'* trainers.

3 Ethan *usually likes / doesn't usually like* Marina's posts.

4 Marina and *Ethan / Ada* want to buy the trainers.

5 Ada *has got some / hasn't got any* purple clothes.

6 Marina tells *Ethan / Ada* the name of a trainers shop.

4 ⭐⭐⭐ Answer the questions with your own ideas.

1 Do you think fashion is important? Why / Why not?

_____

_____

2 Where do you get your ideas about what to wear? For example, from online diaries, friends, magazines, the TV, films, shops?

_____

_____

LANGUAGE IN ACTION
Present continuous

1 ⭐⭐ **Write the words in the correct order to make sentences.**

1 on TV / I'm / fashion show / a / watching

I'm watching a fashion show on TV.

2 her / She / isn't / doing / homework

_____

3 the park / sitting / Marina / is / in

_____

4 a / Ethan / isn't / cap / wearing

_____

5 playing / We're / football

_____

6 same / skirt / the / buying / They're

_____

2 ⭐⭐ **Complete the message with the correct form of the verb *be*.**

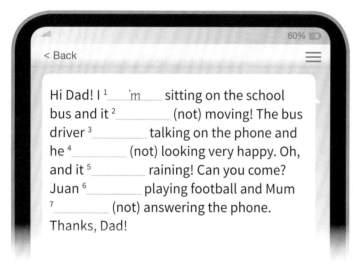

Hi Dad! I ¹___'m___ sitting on the school bus and it ²_____ (not) moving! The bus driver ³_____ talking on the phone and he ⁴_____ (not) looking very happy. Oh, and it ⁵_____ raining! Can you come? Juan ⁶_____ playing football and Mum ⁷_____ (not) answering the phone. Thanks, Dad!

3 ⭐⭐ **What are they doing? Look at pictures 1–4 and write sentences using the words in boxes a and b.**

a dance ~~read~~ ride write

b ~~a magazine~~ salsa on the board a bike

1 *He's reading a magazine.*
2 _____
3 _____
4 _____

4 ⭐⭐ **Match questions 1–6 with answers a–f.**

1 Are you listening to me? 〔b〕
2 Is Anton wearing his new trainers? 〔 〕
3 Is Claudia studying? 〔 〕
4 What are they eating? 〔 〕
5 Which film is Pedro watching? 〔 〕
6 Where are you having your lunch? 〔 〕

a *Wonder Woman*.
b ~~Yes, I am~~!
c In the canteen.
d No, she isn't.
e Fried spiders. Yuck!
f Yes, he is.

5 ⭐⭐⭐ **Answer the questions.**

1 What are you wearing today?

_____

2 What is your best friend doing now?

_____

6 ⭐⭐⭐ **Find out what two people in your family are doing now. Write sentences in the present continuous.**

My sister's watching TV.

_____

_____

_____

①   ②

③   ④

VOCABULARY AND LISTENING

Accessories

1 ⭐ **Complete the accessory words in the spidergram.**

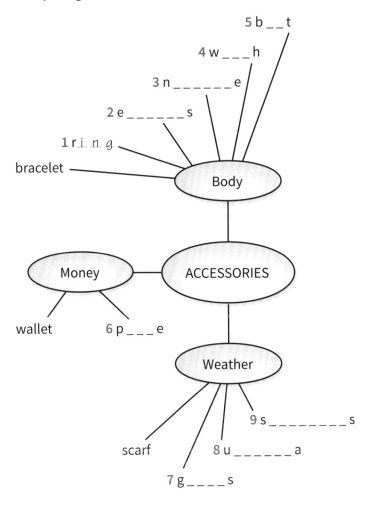

5 b _ _ t
4 w _ _ _ h
3 n _ _ _ _ _ _ e
2 e _ _ _ _ _ _ s
1 r i n g
bracelet
Body

Money
ACCESSORIES

wallet
6 p _ _ _ e

Weather

scarf
9 s _ _ _ _ _ _ _ s
8 u _ _ _ _ _ _ a
7 g _ _ _ _ s

2 ⭐⭐ **Complete the sentences with words from Exercise 1.**

1 Those new jeans look big. You need a
    _____belt_____ .
2 José always wears _____ when it's sunny.
3 Miriam doesn't use a wallet for her money. She uses a _____ .
4 I don't wear a _____ because there's a clock in the classroom.
5 It's raining and I haven't got my _____ !
6 In cold weather, my grandma always wears _____ and a _____ .
7 My dad has a big _____ , but he's never got any money in it!

An interview

🎧 **3** ⭐ **Listen to the interview. Tick (✓) the two things that Alba paints.**
5.01

① □

② □

③ □

🎧 **4** ⭐⭐⭐ **Listen again. Answer the questions.**
5.01

1 Who is Alba painting this week?
   Her baby brother.
2 Where does she get her ideas from?
   _____
3 What does she put in the mini boxes?
   _____
4 What is inside the box for her friend?
   _____
5 What does the interviewer want?
   _____

5 ⭐ **Alba is making you a box (big or small). Write two things you want to put in it. Use the ideas below or your own ideas.**

| a bracelet a ring a wallet a watch gloves |

I'd like _____ and _____ .

LANGUAGE IN ACTION
Present simple and present continuous

1 ⭐ (Circle) the correct options.

1 We use the present *simple* / *continuous* to talk about things happening now.

2 We use the present *simple* / *continuous* to talk about facts, habits and routines.

2 ⭐ Complete the table with the words and phrases in the box.

> at the moment   every Monday   never
> now   ~~on Fridays~~   sometimes   this week
> this morning   today   usually

Facts, habits and routines	Things happening now
on Fridays	

3 ⭐⭐ Write sentences with the present simple or present continuous.

1 Some people / wear / sports clothes / at the weekend

   Some people wear sports clothes at the weekend.

2 I / look for / some jeans / right now

_____

3 They / make / the costumes for the show / now

_____

4 Naima / usually / buy / red clothes

_____

5 We / never / go shopping / on Saturdays

_____

6 A lot of people / wear / hats / at the moment

_____

4 ⭐⭐ Complete the conversation with the present simple or present continuous form of the verbs in brackets.

DANA   What [1] _are you doing_ (do), Paula?

PAULA   I [2] _____ (look) at my clothes. Some of them are very small now. I [3] _____ (often / need) new clothes in the summer.

DANA   Oh! Can I have this skirt?

PAULA   Well, I [4] _____ (always / give) my small clothes to my little sister, but she [5] _____ (not wear) skirts, so it's yours!

DANA   Thanks! Where [6] _____ (you / usually / buy) your clothes?

PAULA   A shop near home. My mum [7] _____ (shop) there right now.

DANA   [8] _____ (they / sell) accessories, too? I [9] _____ (look for) a bracelet at the moment.

PAULA   Yes, they do! They [10] _____ (sell) lovely bracelets. We can go shopping there together next time!

5 ⭐⭐⭐ Answer the questions.

1 What do you do with your old clothes and accessories?

_____

2 What clothes are you wearing a lot at the moment?

_____

3 What do you usually wear in the evening during the week?

_____

WRITING
A description of a photo

1 ⭐ **Read the description and look at the photo. Write the names of the people (a–e).**

a   Damir   d _____

b _____   e _____

c _____

A photo of a day out

By Alyssa

1   This is a photo of my friends and me. We're on a school trip to a national park. It's cold but sunny.

2   The boy on the left is Damir. He ¹*looks* / (*'s looking*) down. He often ²*looks* / *is looking* down because he hates photos! He ³*wears* / *'s wearing* a black and grey hoodie. Next to Damirl is Peter. He's in a pink shirt and a grey jumper. The boys ⁴*don't wear* / *aren't wearing* jackets in the photo. Then that's me in the middle, with a jacket and a checked shirt. Carmen's next to me. She ⁵*wears* / *'s wearing* her favourite denim jacket and a big scarf. Gina's on the right. She's got a grey T-shirt, a green jacket and a scarf. Gina's the only one in a hat.

3   This is one of my favourite photos. We ⁶*laugh* / *'re laughing* because it's a fun day. I like this photo because there are trees at the back and we all look happy. We always ⁷*have* / *are having* a great time!

2 ⭐⭐ Ⓒircle **the correct form of the verbs (1–7) in the description.**

3 ⭐⭐ **Read the description again. Complete the sentences with the words in the box.**

> Alyssa   boys   girls   Peter   ~~trees~~

1 The _____ trees _____ are at the back.

2 _____ is in the middle. Carmen and _____ are next to her.

3 The _____ are on the left.

4 The _____ are on the right.

4 ⭐⭐ **Match topics a–c with paragraphs 1–3.**

a why it is a favourite photo   ☐

b people in the photo, where they are, what they're wearing   ☐

c who is in the photo and where the photo is   ☐

Write your own description of a photo of a day out.

PLAN

5 ⭐⭐ **Choose your photo and make notes. Decide what information to include in each paragraph. Use the information in Exercise 4 to help you.**

WRITE

6 ⭐⭐⭐ **Write your description. Remember to include the information in the correct order, the present simple and present continuous, and expressions from the *Useful language* box (see Student's Book, p65).**

CHECK

7 **Do you …**

- describe the people in the photo, including the clothes and accessories they are wearing?
- describe the people's positions in the photo?
- say why you like the photo?

5 REVIEW

VOCABULARY

1 (Circle) the odd one out.

1 joggers / T-shirt / jeans
2 trainers / shorts / boots
3 shorts / boots / skirt
4 jacket / hoodie / cap
5 shirt / skirt / shorts
6 flip-flops / boots / trainers

2 Complete the crossword. Use the pictures.

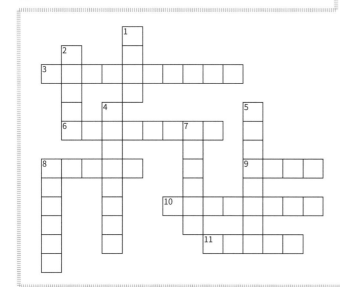

LANGUAGE IN ACTION

3 Complete the sentences with the present continuous form of the verbs in the box.

| do   look   make   not rain |
| not wear   watch |

1 **A:** What _____ you _____ now?
  B: I'm doing my homework.
2 At the moment, I _____ for a new jacket with my dad.
3 They _____ a TV programme about the history of fashion.
4 We _____ our school uniform today – it's Sunday.
5 My grandma _____ me a new dress for my birthday.
6 You don't need an umbrella. It _____ .

ACROSS →

3   6   8

9   10   11

DOWN ↓

1   2   4

5   7   8

4 (Circle) the correct options.

MAYA What ¹*do you usually do / are you usually doing* at the weekend?

ISAAC We ²*sometimes visit / are sometimes visiting* my grandparents, but they ³*travel / 're travelling* around Europe at the moment.

LILY ⁴*Is Jimi having / Does Jimi have* lunch at home this month?

TOM Yes. He usually ⁵*has / is having* lunch at school, but this month he ⁶*goes / 's going* home early.

HUGO ⁷*Does Dad do / Is Dad doing* the shopping now?

CALEB No, it's Sunday. The shops ⁸*close / are closing* early on Sundays.

CUMULATIVE LANGUAGE

5 Complete the conversation with the missing words. (Circle) the correct options.

ADIL Hi, Mum. ¹_____ are you?

MUM Hi, Adil! I'm ²_____ the shopping with Dad.

ADIL Oh, OK! Listen, ³_____ for a bike ride this afternoon with Tom and his brother?

MUM Sure! We haven't got ⁴_____ plans.

ADIL Great! But ⁵_____ a problem. I can't ⁶_____ my trainers, or my hoodie. Where are they?

MUM I ⁷_____ know. They're your things.

ADIL Oh! The trainers are under my bed, but I can't see my hoodie. Can you buy ⁸_____ a new one, please?

MUM A new one? I haven't got ⁹_____ time now, and you've got a hoodie! You need to look for ¹⁰_____.

ADIL Ugh! I hate ¹¹_____ things.

MUM I know, but how often ¹²_____ things when you look for them?

ADIL Hmm, I suppose so. OK, speak later.

1 a When	b Where	c What
2 a does	b do	c doing
3 a can I go	b I can go	c do I go
4 a any	b some	c a
5 a there are	b there's	c it's
6 a find	b to find	c finding
7 a not	b 'm not	c don't
8 a me	b it	c my
9 a many	b any	c a lot
10 a it	b they	c them
11 a look for	b looking for	c looks for
12 a are you finding	b do you find	c you find

SPORT FOR LIFE

VOCABULARY
Sports

1 ⭐ **Complete the word puzzle. Use the pictures (1–12). What is the mystery word in grey?**

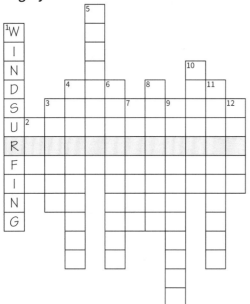

¹W
I
N
D
S
U
R
F
I
N
G

2 ⭐⭐ **Complete the rules with *play*, *do* or *go*.**

We usually use ¹_____ with sports that end in *-ing*.
We usually use ²_____ with ball sports.
We usually use ³_____ with other sports.

3 ⭐⭐ (Circle) **the correct options.**

I like doing sport. At school, we do ¹*running* / (*athletics*) and I like that. Sometimes at the weekend I go ²*swimming* / *yoga* with my brother. He does ³*gymnastics* / *rugby* at an after-school club and goes ⁴*running* / *table tennis* twice a week. I don't really like team sports, but in the holidays I sometimes play ⁵*sailing* / *volleyball* with my friends on the beach. And I love going ⁶*yoga* / *rock climbing* with my dad in the mountains.

4 ⭐⭐⭐ **Answer the questions.**

1 What are your favourite sports?

_____

2 Do you do sports at school? Which sports?

_____

Explore it! 🖱️

Guess the correct answer.
Which sport comes from Canada?
a ice hockey   b table tennis   c rugby
Find an interesting fact about sport in your country. Then send a question in an email to a classmate or ask them it in the next class.

READING
Online FAQs

1 ⭐ **Read the article. What sport is it about? Tick (✓) the correct photo (1–3).**

FUN IN THE SUN!

Are you looking for a new sport? Do you want to try something more exciting? In New Zealand we've got the answer – try zorbing! It's new and it's different!

FAQs

Q1:
What is Zorbing?

Zorbing is a fun outdoor sport. It's more popular here in New Zealand than in other countries.

Q2: _____

You need a large plastic ball. This is called a zorb. You get inside the ball and run or walk. When you move, the ball moves, too! You know where you're going and how you're moving because you can see through the ball. Lots of people love going down a hill in their zorb. It's exciting!

Q3: _____

No, it's an individual sport. You get inside the zorb on your own, but it's good fun to go with family or friends because you can have races – sometimes children are faster than their parents!

Q4: _____

Yes, it is, but always do it in a zorbing centre and follow the rules. Have fun, but be careful – don't get hurt!

Q5: _____

Yes. To go zorbing, you usually need to be six years old or older.

Q6: _____

There are zorbing centres in many places on the South Island. Click here for a list of centres.

Q7: _____

Yes, it's more expensive than other traditional sports, but it's a great activity for special days. So, are you ready for zorbing? What are you waiting for!

2 ⭐⭐ **Read the article again. Complete it with the missing questions.**

a Is there an age limit?
b Is it a team sport?
c What do you do?
d ~~What is zorbing?~~
e Where can I do it?
f Is it expensive?
g Is it safe?

3 ⭐⭐ **Read the article again and underline these words. Then check their meaning in a dictionary and complete the sentences.**

> get hurt   hill   race   ~~safe~~   try

1 Be careful! Going out alone at night isn't ___safe___ .
2 The Spartathlon is a _____ in Greece. People run 246 kilometres!
3 I live at the top of a _____ . Walking down to school is easy!
4 I love tennis, but this year I want to _____ a new sport.
5 Careful there! You can fall and _____ !

4 ⭐⭐⭐ **Answer the questions.**

1 Do you want to try zorbing? Why / Why not?

_____
_____
_____

2 What fun outdoor sports are popular in your country?

_____
_____
_____

LANGUAGE IN ACTION
Comparatives

1 ⭐ **Write the comparative forms.**

1 small
   smaller

2 big
   _____

3 good
   _____

4 happy
   _____

5 interesting
   _____

6 bad
   _____

2 ⭐ **Complete the rules with the adjectives from Exercise 1.**

1 For one-syllable adjectives, add -er:
   _____smaller_____ .

2 For two-syllable adjectives ending in -y, remove the -y and add -ier: _____ .

3 For long adjectives, add *more* to the adjective: _____ .

4 For one-syllable adjectives ending in a vowel and a consonant, double the consonant and add -er: _____ .

5 For irregular adjectives, use a different word: _____ and _____ .

3 ⭐⭐ <u>Underline</u> **and correct one mistake in each sentence.**

1 Windsurfing is more expensive <u>that</u> running. _____than_____

2 Rugby is more fast than basketball.
   _____

3 Runners are usually thiner than swimmers.
   _____

4 Which sport is noisyer, volleyball or yoga?
   _____

5 She's badder at gymnastics than at hockey.
   _____

6 Playing sport is more better than watching it. _____

4 ⭐⭐ **Complete the sentences with the comparative form of the adjectives in brackets.**

1 An ice hockey match is _____longer_____ than a basketball match. (long)

2 I think rock climbing is _____ than yoga. (exciting)

3 Lola's _____ at tennis than her dad. (good)

4 Our school hockey team is _____ than the rugby team. (bad)

5 We think rugby is a _____ game than football. (difficult)

6 Doing sport is _____ than watching TV. (healthy)

5 ⭐⭐ **Complete the questions with a comparative adjective. Then check the answers at the bottom of the page.**

DANIEL Let's do this quiz! First question: Which ball is ¹_____faster_____, a table tennis or a tennis ball?

ANDREA A table tennis ball?

DANIEL Next question: Which match is ²_____, a basketball or an ice hockey match?

ANDREA I don't know. Ice hockey?

DANIEL Number three: Which country is ³_____ at table tennis, China or South Korea?

ANDREA South Korea, I think.

DANIEL And the last question: Which sport is ⁴_____ at schools here in New Zealand, hockey or athletics?

ANDREA Oh, dear! I don't know. Athletics maybe. What are the answers?

6 ⭐⭐⭐ **Write three sentences comparing sports. Look at Exercise 4 to help you.**

<u>I think football is more entertaining than rugby.</u>

_____

_____

_____

Answers

1 table tennis ball: 116 km/h; tennis ball: 263 km/h

2 ice hockey match: 60 minutes; basketball match: 48 minutes

3 China (1); South Korea (2)

4 number of people playing at schools in New Zealand: hockey: 13,967, athletics: 12,713

VOCABULARY AND LISTENING
Sports verbs

1 ⭐ Match photos 1–6 with six of the sports verbs a–l.

> a dive b kick ~~c bounce~~ d hit e catch f climb
> g jump h lift i pass j run k throw l score

 1 c

 2

 3

 4

 5

 6

2 ⭐⭐ Circle the correct verbs.

I don't understand rugby! OK, the players
¹*pass* / *score* the ball to each other. Then they
²*catch* / *run* up the field and put the ball over a
line to ³*score* / *hit* points. They also ⁴*kick* / *jump*
the ball over a big goalpost. But sometimes the
teams make a circle and push each other. Then
one player ⁵*scores* / *throws* the ball into the
circle and another player from the same team
gets it. And sometimes some players ⁶*lift* / *jump*
on top of other players!

3 ⭐⭐⭐ Write two sentences describing what
players can and can't do in a sport. Use the sports
verbs from Exercise 1.

In football, the players can kick the ball but they can't
score goals with their hands. _____

A conversation

🎧 **4** ⭐ **6.01** Look at the photo and listen to a
conversation about goalball, a sport for blind
people. Circle the correct answers.

1 Goalball players use a special ball with *lights* /
   sound.
2 Goalball is *a team* / *an individual* sport.

🎧 **5** ⭐⭐⭐ **6.01** Listen again. Complete the sentences
with one word.

1 Blind people can usually hear sounds
   ___better___ than other people.
2 The goalball ball is like a _____ , but
   heavier.
3 A goalball team has _____ players in it.
4 Players try to _____ the ball to score a
   goal.
5 They use their _____ to stop the ball.
6 Some players throw the ball at _____
   kilometres per hour.
7 Jon plays goalball on a _____ court.
8 The boy wants to watch Jon's match on
   _____ .

6 ⭐⭐⭐ Watch part of a Paralympics goalball
match on the internet. Then write three things
you like about it.

I like how the players throw the ball. _____

LANGUAGE IN ACTION
Superlatives

1 ⭐ **Complete the table with the superlative form of the adjectives in the box.**

bad ~~entertaining~~ fit healthy old

The most + adjective	The + double the final consonant + -est	The + change y to i + -est	The + adjective + -est	The + irregular form
the most popular	2 _____	the easiest	4 _____	the best
1 the most entertaining	the biggest	3 _____	the fastest	5 _____

2 ⭐⭐ **Complete the text with the superlative form of the adjectives in brackets.**

My cousin Nick is the
¹ most popular (popular)
person in my family. He's the
² _____ (tall) of my cousins
and also the ³ _____ (fit) –
at the weekend, he does yoga and plays hockey!
Everybody loves Nick.

He's the ⁴ _____ (happy) person
I know! I'm the ⁵ _____ (young)
person in my family and the
⁶ _____ (bad) at sport! But that's
OK because we're all different. I love
reading and writing stories. Nick says I write the
⁷ _____ (interesting) stories in the world.

3 ⭐⭐ **Write the questions in the quiz using the superlative form of the adjectives. Then (circle) the correct answers. Check your answers at the bottom of the quiz!**

SPORTS QUESTION TIME!

1 Which is / popular / sport in Brazil?
Which is the most popular sport in Brazil?
a basketball   **b** football

2 Which is one of the / old / ball sports?
_____
a Ulama. It comes from Mexico.
b Alama. It comes from Ecuador.

3 Which is one of the / new / sports?
_____
a table tennis.
b 360Ball. You use a racket and a ball and play it in a round field.

4 Which is one of the / difficult / sports for many people?
_____
a rock climbing   **b** running

5 Which is one of the / expensive / sports in the world?
_____
a tennis   **b** swimming

ANSWERS
1 b **2** a **3** b **4** a **5** a

4 ⭐⭐⭐ **Complete the questions with the superlative form of the adjectives. Then answer them for you.**

1 Who is the youngest (young) person in your family?
_____

2 Which is _____ (popular) sport at your school?
_____

3 Which is _____ (difficult) school subject?
_____

4 Which is _____ (entertaining) film you know?
_____

WRITING
A profile of a sportsperson

1 ★ **Look at the photos and read the profile. Then complete the sentence.**

For Ivan, Natalia Partyka is an _____ sportsperson because she plays table tennis with _____ .

A popular sportsperson from my country

By Ivan Nowak

1 I'm from Poland and I think one of the ¹*more / most* popular sportspeople from my country is Natalia Partyka. She's a table tennis player. She's 1.73 m tall and weighs 64 kg. She's only got one hand and part of her right arm.

2 Natalia trains for about six hours a day. She often plays with her ²*older / more older* sister, Sandra. Sometimes she practises bouncing the ball on the top part of her arm to begin the game. In her free time, Natalia loves reading the letters from her fans. She also likes going to the beach with her friends.

3 I think Natalia is the ³*more / most* amazing sportsperson from my country because she plays with one hand. She's also an excellent athlete – she's part of the Paralympic team and the Olympic Games team, too. She's got more gold medals than any other table tennis player in Poland and she's one of the ⁴*most / more* successful players in the world, too.

2 ★★ (Circle) the correct options (1–4) in the profile.

3 ★★ Read the profile again. <u>Underline</u> two sentences with *also* and two sentences with *too*. Then complete the rules with *also* or *too*.

We use *too* and *also* to give extra information. We use ¹_____ at the end of a sentence. We use ²_____ after the verb *be* and before other verbs.

4 ★★ Read the profile again. Match topics a–c with paragraphs 1–3.

a training and other interests ☐

b achievements ☐

c basic information and description ☐

Write a profile of a popular sportsperson from your country.

PLAN

5 ★★ **Make notes about the sportsperson. Decide what information to include in each paragraph. Use the information in Exercise 4 to help you.**

WRITE

6 ★★★ **Write your profile. Remember to include three paragraphs, comparatives and superlatives and expressions from the *Useful language* box (see Student's Book, p77).**

CHECK

7 **Do you …**
- give basic information and a description of your sportsperson?
- describe their sport using sports verbs?
- talk about their achievements and why you like them?

VOCABULARY

1 Complete the table with the sports in the box.

> athletics   hockey   rugby
> running   sailing   swimming   tennis
> windsurfing   yoga

Water sports	Ball sports	Other sports

2 Find 12 sports verbs in the word search.

B	D	I	B	T	D	I	V	E	H
U	I	C	S	D	Q	H	G	R	I
V	0	L	I	F	T	A	H	B	T
Y	K	I	C	K	R	Z	O	S	P
E	C	M	W	Q	M	N	S	C	A
N	P	B	O	U	N	C	E	O	L
L	Y	K	J	C	J	A	T	R	U
T	H	R	O	W	V	T	G	E	R
H	J	U	M	P	W	C	E	F	U
F	P	A	S	S	K	H	X	G	N

3 Complete the sentences with the correct form of the verbs from Exercise 2.

1 A table tennis player b_____ the ball across the table.

2 My brother loves j_____ on the bed!

3 Mount Everest, the highest mountain in the world, is very difficult to c_____.

4 We never s_____ many goals in football.

5 Tennis players can't h_____ the ball with their hands. They use a racket.

6 In gymnastics, we sometimes l_____ heavy boxes to make our arms strong.

LANGUAGE IN ACTION

4 Write sentences using the comparative form of the adjectives in brackets.

1 zorbing / running (exciting)

_____

2 water / fizzy drinks (healthy)

_____

3 joggers / jeans (comfortable)

_____

4 a table tennis ball / a tennis ball (small)

_____

5 jumping / rock climbing (easy)

_____

5 Complete the text with the superlative form of the adjectives in brackets.

I think tennis is the ¹_____ (boring) sport, but my dad loves it! At the moment, he's in London at the All England Club. This club is the ²_____ (old) in the world. Every year, there are different tennis tournaments there. The ³_____ (popular) one is called Wimbledon. My dad says all the ⁴_____ (good) players want to win there. People watching tennis at Wimbledon don't usually speak to each other a lot. The ⁵_____ (bad) thing you can do at Wimbledon is talk! The players don't like noise. I think the ⁶_____ (easy) thing is to watch Wimbledon on TV, but not for me – I prefer a good film!

CUMULATIVE LANGUAGE

6 Complete the conversation with the missing words. (Circle) the correct options.

ESMA	Which sports ¹_____ you like, Rafael?
RAFAEL	I like ²_____ athletics and playing football.
ESMA	I think football is the ³_____ sport in the world.
RAFAEL	Me, too! Today I ⁴_____ football training and then yoga.
ESMA	Yoga! I think it's ⁵_____ than athletics!
RAFAEL	Then try it with me! I can teach you the ⁶_____ exercises.
ESMA	Sounds great, but I'm the ⁷_____ student in the world!
RAFAEL	Ah! But I'm a ⁸_____ teacher!
ESMA	OK! I ⁹_____ try.
RAFAEL	¹⁰_____ your joggers in your bag?
ESMA	No, but I can ¹¹_____ home and get them now.
RAFAEL	Perfect. Run home and bring ¹²_____ joggers!

1	a	does	b	are	c	do
2	a	does	b	do	c	doing
3	a	best	b	better	c	good
4	a	got	b	've got	c	'm got
5	a	most interesting	b	more interesting	c	interesting
6	a	more easy	b	easier	c	easiest
7	a	bad	b	worse	c	worst
8	a	good	b	the better	c	best
9	a	can	b	have	c	do
10	a	Have you got	b	You got	c	You have
11	a	go to	b	go	c	come
12	a	yours	b	you	c	your

7 AMAZING ANIMALS

VOCABULARY
Animals

1 ⭐ **Find 13 more words for animals in the word search.**

C	R	O	C	O	D	I	L	E	D	E	Y
H	I	P	P	O	B	D	O	N	K	E	Y
J	L	S	I	S	W	A	Y	U	K	A	G
P	H	W	B	C	N	G	D	N	T	G	I
A	M	H	E	K	M	A	N	I	J	L	R
R	Q	O	A	V	I	D	K	T	H	E	A
R	K	R	R	P	L	U	Z	E	B	C	F
O	R	S	O	E	N	C	D	W	V	E	F
T	X	E	G	T	W	K	M	O	U	S	E
Z	F	W	H	A	L	E	S	K	S	B	A
A	N	F	M	P	B	M	O	N	K	E	Y
L	I	O	N	S	T	C	N	U	I	J	X

2 ⭐ **Circle the animal in each category which is not correct. Then add a different animal to each category in the list.**

1 **Birds**	2 **Mammals**	3 **Reptiles**
duck	eagle	snake
hippo	giraffe	bear
parrot	lion	crocodile
___	___	___

3 ⭐⭐ **Read the descriptions and write the names of the animals from Exercise 1.**

1 This animal is a mammal. It usually lives in forests and cold places. It's very big and has lots of hair.
    bear

2 This animal lives in water in hot countries. It's a reptile with a big mouth and lots of big teeth.
    _____

3 This is a bird. It eats plants and it can swim and fly. It usually lives near water. _____

4 This animal likes cheese a lot but it doesn't like cats! It's usually grey and has lots of babies.
    _____

5 This animal eats meat. It hasn't got any legs. Some of them can kill other animals and sometimes people, too. _____

6 This is a very large sea mammal. It has a hole on the top of its head. _____

4 ⭐⭐ **Choose another animal from Exercise 1 and write a definition.**

1 This animal is _____
_____

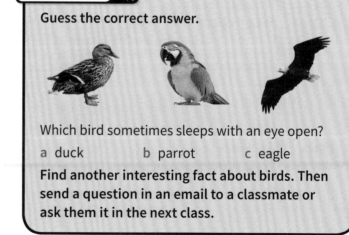

Explore it! 🖱️

Guess the correct answer.

Which bird sometimes sleeps with an eye open?

a duck   b parrot   c eagle

Find another interesting fact about birds. Then send a question in an email to a classmate or ask them it in the next class.

READING

Fact files

1 ⭐ **Read the fact file below and (circle) the correct answers.**

1 Polar bears weigh …
   a about 360 kg.　　b about 560 kg.

2 Polar bears live in …
   a the Arctic.　　b the Antarctic.

3 Polar bears eat … of seal in a week.
   a about 35 kg　　b about 55 kg

POLAR BEAR

Weight: about 360 kg
Habitat: the Arctic
Food: seals
Fact: Polar bears can smell a seal 32 km away!
They can eat 55 kg of seal in a week.

2 ⭐ **Read the article. What's special about the town of Churchill?** _____

3 ⭐⭐ **Read the article again and <u>underline</u> these words. Then check their meaning in a dictionary and complete the sentences.**

> attack　escape　hunt　~~ice~~　male　prison

1 In winter, there is ___ice___ on the river.

2 A female animal is a girl and a _____ is a boy.

3 People can go to _____ for killing an elephant.

4 Hungry lions are dangerous and they sometimes _____ people.

5 Whales often _____ other mammals, like seals, at night.

6 The man saw the polar bear in the street and ran into a shop to _____ .

Polar bears are in town!

Churchill is a small town on the Hudson Bay in Canada. Every October, November and December, it has some special visitors: polar bears! They can't hunt seals until it is colder and there is more ice, so they visit the town looking for food.

From October to December in 2016, there were 800 people living in Churchill and 10,000 tourists. The tourists were there to see the polar bears – there were more than 1,000 bears.

Some bears attack people, so the police ask people to be careful and to leave their cars open in the town centre. Then people can jump inside if they need to escape an angry bear! To keep people safe, the police sometimes put angry bears in prison for a few days. Then they take them out of the town.

People in the town say the worst year was 1983. On 29th November, a young male bear killed a man in the city centre. This was the first attack for many years. In 2013, a large bear attacked a man in the street. The bear was put in prison and the man went to the doctor's, but he was fine after a few days.

4 ⭐⭐ **Read the article again. Are the sentences _T_ (true) or _F_ (false)? Correct the false sentences.**

1 Polar bears visit the town every August.
   F. Polar bears visit the town from October to December.

2 The polar bears go to the town because it's colder there.
   _____

3 When the polar bears are angry, people can hide in cars.
   _____

4 When the polar bears attack people, they go to prison.
   _____

5 ⭐⭐⭐ **Answer the questions with your own ideas.**

1 What do you think the polar bears eat in Churchill?
   _____

2 Do you think the food they eat in Churchill is good for them? Why / Why not?
   _____

LANGUAGE IN ACTION
was/were, there was/were

1 ⭐ (Circle) **the correct options.**

1 The polar bears *was* /(*were*) in Churchill in
November because (*there wasn't*) / *there weren't*
enough food for them to eat in the river.

2 In the past, the weather *was* / *were* always cold in
November and *there was* / *there were* a lot
of ice on the river.

3 When it *was* / *were* colder, *there was* / *there were*
seals for the polar bears to eat in the river.

4 In the past *there was* / *there were* more ice because
the temperatures *wasn't* / *weren't* as high.

2 ⭐ **Match the questions with the answers.**

1 Was it hotter in the past? ☐ a Yes, there were.
2 Were they wild animals? ☐ b No, there wasn't.
3 Was there ice in summer? ☐ c Yes, they were.
4 Were there seals? ☐ d No, it wasn't.

3 ⭐⭐ **Complete the text with *was(n't)* / *were(n't)*.**

Thousands of years ago there were
mammoths in Europe. They ¹ _were_
large mammals with very big tusks.
They ² _____ very strong. They
³ _____ like the elephants we see
today because they ⁴ _____ much
bigger and had fur. The sabre-toothed
tiger also lived in Europe at the same
time. It ⁵ _____ really a tiger, it
⁶ _____ a big cat. Its teeth
⁷ _____ very long and it
⁸ _____ a very dangerous animal.

4 ⭐⭐ **Complete the text with the correct form of**
there was or *there were*.

When I was a girl, I lived in South Africa. Around my house
¹ _there wasn't_ a lot to do but ² _____ lots of animals to
see because we lived next to a wildlife park. In my bedroom
³ _____ a big window, and in the mornings, I could see
lots of animals. ⁴ _____ hippos in the water and
⁵ _____ enormous elephants sleeping. ⁶ _____
always a big giraffe next to a tree and a strange bird sitting on
the tree that looked angry! My favourite animals are tigers, but
⁷ _____ any tigers in the wildlife park. That's because
there are no tigers in South Africa. ⁸ _____ a lot of
time to see the animals because I was at school all day, but
I remember all of them.

5 ⭐⭐ **Put the words in the correct order to make questions.**
Then write answers for you in your notebook.

1 were / Where / on Saturday / you / ?
Where were you on Saturday?

2 your / favourite / six / What / was / animal / when / you / were / ?
What was _____

3 people / were / there / How / many / last year / your / class / in / ?
How many _____

4 in 2011 / were / you / How / old / ?
How old _____

5 your town / in / Was / there / were / you / when / young / a zoo / ?
Was there _____

6 ⭐⭐⭐ **Find out about an animal from the past, like mammoths**
or sabre-toothed tigers. Write three sentences about them. Use
was and *were*.

_____

_____

VOCABULARY AND LISTENING
Adjectives

1 ☆ **Choose the correct letters to complete the adjectives.**

a c d f̶ g i l n r u v y

1 beauti f ul
2 cle__er
3 __ute
4 dan__erous

5 heav__
6 l__zy
7 wil__
8 no__sy

9 ti__y
10 la__ge
11 q__iet
12 __ong

2 ☆☆ **Complete the text with adjectives from Exercise 1.**

I've got a ¹ _beautiful_ little cat. He's got a lovely face and I think he's really ² _____ . He's ³ _____ too and can do lots of tricks. My mum likes him because he doesn't make a lot of noise like some pets. She says he's very ⁴ _____ . He can't run fast because his legs aren't very ⁵ _____ ! I prefer small pets because some of my friends' big pets are ⁶ _____ and they make me nervous.

3 ☆☆☆ **Which pets have your family or friends got? Use the adjectives and your own ideas to write four sentences.**

My best friend has got a tiny mouse.

_____

_____

_____

A class discussion

🎧 4 ☆ **Listen to a teacher talking about wolves with her class.** (Circle) **the correct answers.**
7.01

1 The teacher is talking about wolves that live in an *American park* / *English zoo*.

2 There weren't any wolves there for *50 / 70* years.

3 There were about *6 / 100* wolves there last year.

🎧 5 ☆☆ **Listen again and answer the questions. Remember the *Learn to Learn* tip: look for the question words and think about the answers before you listen.**
7.01

1 How does one student describe wolves?
They are fast, dangerous and clever.

2 Why weren't there any wolves in Yellowstone Park for 70 years?

_____

_____

3 How many wolves were in the park about 20 years ago?

_____

_____

4 Why was it difficult for the wolves at first?

_____

5 Why is it difficult to see wolves in the park?

_____

_____

6 ☆☆☆ **Which other wild animals do you think live in Yellowstone Park? Write some ideas below.**

_____

_____

_____

LANGUAGE IN ACTION
Past simple: regular and irregular verbs

1 ⭐ **Write the infinitive of these past tense verbs.**

1 had	_have_	5 heard	_____	9 shared	_____
2 slept	_____	6 saw	_____	10 wanted	_____
3 took	_____	7 became	_____	11 found	_____
4 looked	_____	8 gave	_____	12 went	_____

2 ⭐⭐ **Complete the sentences with the correct past simple form of the verbs in the box.**

look	~~not give~~	have	not want
sleep	not find	see	not go

1 You __didn't give__ the donkey its food.

2 We _____ lots of snakes at the wildlife park.

3 The horse _____ to eat my apple. It wasn't hungry.

4 They _____ for the cat in the garden but they _____ him.

5 My dad _____ a parrot as a pet when he was a child.

6 The cat _____ out, she _____ on my bed all day.

3 ⭐⭐ **Write the words in the correct order to make sentences.**

1 park / years / The / 20 / safari / opened / ago

The safari park opened 20 years ago.

2 Crocodiles / killed / year / 1,000 / people / last

_____

3 bears / days / in town / ago / Two / three / were / there

_____

4 blue / last / saw / whales / summer / They

_____

5 an / The / home / hour / cat / came / ago

_____

4 ⭐⭐⭐ **Complete the text with the past simple form of the verbs in brackets.**

Flo, a dog from Northern Ireland, disappeared in October 2011. The Gallaghers, Flo's family, [1] _looked_ (look) for her but they [2] _____ (not find) her. They were very sad. Then in 2014, a volunteer at the local animal hospital [3] _____ (hear) about a dog with no home. The dog [4] _____ (sleep) in an old building about ten miles from the Gallaghers' house. The volunteers at the hospital [5] _____ (not want) the dog to stay there. They [6] _____ (go) to find her. Soon the dog [7] _____ (have) a new home at the animal hospital, and they [8] _____ (share) photos of her on Facebook. The Gallagher family [9] _____ (see) the photos and [10] _____ (become) very excited – it was Flo! The next day they [11] _____ (take) her home. They [12] _____ (give) her a big dinner.

WRITING

A biography

1 ⭐ Look at the photos and read the biography. Which animals did Jack help?

Jack Oliver

1 Jack Oliver was born in Australia ¹(in) / on 1978. His family started an animal sanctuary to give animals a safe place to live. ²When / At Jack was five, he found a three-metre snake in his garden! It was injured! Jack and his parents decided to look after it. Jack helped at the sanctuary and he became an animal expert.

2 Jack met his wife Alison ³on / in 2003. They had a daughter called Ava. ⁴In / On 2005, Jack started to make TV programmes with a local TV channel. He filmed several series at his family's sanctuary. He also went to other countries to find and help injured animals. He helped to make them better and find a

safe place for them to live. ⁵In / On 25th September, 2012, Jack had an accident with a crocodile but he survived.

3 Jack's wife and daughter help with his work. A few weeks ⁶when / ago, Ava found an injured duck and decided to take it to her father's sanctuary. She helped her father to look after it. Ava wants to be an animal expert one day, just like her father!

2 ⭐⭐ ⟨Circle⟩ the correct prepositions (1–6) in the biography.

3 ⭐⭐ Read the biography again and write the events in the box in the timeline below.

| met Alison   ~~born~~   found a snake |
| crocodile attack   TV programmes |

⟵──────────────────────⟶

  1978   1983   2003   2005   2012

1 _born_   3 _____   5 _____

      2 _____   4 _____

4 ⭐⭐ Match headings a–c with paragraphs 1–3.

a Now ☐
b Early life ☐
c Main events ☐

Write a biography about a person who works with animals.

PLAN

5 ⭐⭐ Think of a famous person who works with animals. Look for information on the internet and create a timeline about his or her life. Use Exercise 3 to help you.

6 Decide what information to include in each paragraph. Use Exercise 4 to help you.

WRITE

7 ⭐⭐⭐ Write your biography. Remember to include three paragraphs, the past simple and time expressions and the *Useful language* expressions (see Student's Book, p89).

CHECK

8 Do you …
- give information from the timeline of your famous person?
- do you write about the events in their life in the correct order?

VOCABULARY

1 Complete the crossword. Use the pictures.

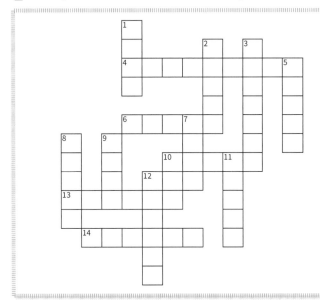

ACROSS

4   6   10

13   14

DOWN

1   2   3

5   7   8

9   11   12

2 Complete the sentences with an adjective from the box.

> lazy   cute   wild   dangerous   clever   quiet
> beautiful   heavy   tiny   large   noisy

1   Kodiak brown bears are very _____ animals, but their babies are _____ – they are only about 23 centimetres long and they weigh only 450 gm.

2   Hippos are very _____ animals. They kill a lot of people.

3   My snake doesn't make much noise. He is very _____ .

4   When blue whales are born, they weigh about 2,700 kg. That's _____ !

5   Male lions are _____ . They sleep and the female lions hunt.

6   African grey parrots can learn 1,000 words. They are really _____ .

7   Howler monkeys are very _____ . You can hear them from 4km away!

8   Baby lions look _____ , but be careful! They are _____ animals, not pets, and can attack you.

9   Oh, I love looking at photos of tigers! I think tigers are really _____ animals.

LANGUAGE IN ACTION

3 (Circle) the correct options in the dialogue.

A   ¹*Was / Were* you at school yesterday?

B   No, I ²*wasn't / weren't*. ³*There were / I was* on a school trip to an aquarium.

A   ⁴*Was it / Was there* good?

B   Fantastic! There ⁵*was / were* hundreds of different fish. My favourites ⁶*were / was* the parrot fish and the clown fish. ⁷*There was / It was* a dolphin area, too.

A   ⁸*Were there / There was* any sharks?

B   Yes, ⁹*they were / there were*, but there ¹⁰*wasn't / weren't* time to go and see them. The aquarium's really big!

4 Complete the text with the past simple form of the verbs in brackets.

Last year I ¹_____ (want) a pet, but I ²_____ (not have) any money so I ³_____ (go) to an animal rescue centre. At the centre I ⁴_____ (see) a lot of animals, but I ⁵_____ (not know) which one I ⁶_____ (like) best. Then I ⁷_____ (hear) a noise in a corner. A tiny white cat ⁸_____ (look) up at me with his big blue eyes. He was really cute. I ⁹_____ (take) him home, and he ¹⁰_____ (become) my best friend.

CUMULATIVE LANGUAGE

5 Complete the conversation with the missing words. (Circle) the correct options.

ISA   Hi, Adela! How ¹_____ your weekend?

ADELA   ²_____ really nice, thanks! On Saturday morning I ³_____ basketball with my team – we ⁴_____ our match.

ISA   No way! Your team always wins!

ADELA   I know, but it ⁵_____ fun to play and we are still at the top of the league table. Anyway on Saturday afternoon I ⁶_____ to a football match with my cousins and my uncle – my team ⁷_____ so I ⁸_____ really happy!

ISA   Wow! Lucky you!

ADELA   Yes, then on Sunday afternoon, I ⁹_____ my friends and we went to the cinema. ¹⁰_____ a great film! The best bit was the burger we ¹¹_____ in a restaurant near the cinema after the film. It was delicious!

ISA   Really? Where's the restaurant?

ADELA   On George Street. Let's go now!

1	a	was	b	are	c	were
2	a	There was	b	There were	c	It was
3	a	plays	b	did play	c	played
4	a	lost	b	losed	c	loses
5	a	were	b	weren't	c	was
6	a	was	b	go	c	went
7	a	wins	b	won	c	win
8	a	wasn't	b	aren't	c	was
9	a	meet	b	meeted	c	met
10	a	It was	b	It weren't	c	It wasn't
11	a	eat	b	eated	c	ate

8 LOST AND FOUND

VOCABULARY
Places in town

1 ⭐ Look at the photos and complete the words for places.

1 s w i m m i n g
  p o o l
2 b _ _ _ _ _ _ _ _
  a _ _ _ _ _
3 p _ _ _ _
  o _ _ _ _ _ _
4 s _ _ _ _ _ _ _
  c _ _ _ _ _
5 a _ _ _ _ _ _ _ _

6 h _ _ _ _ _ _ _ _
7 s _ _ _ _ _ _ _ _
  c _ _ _ _ _ _
8 c _ _ _
  p _ _ _ _
9 c _ _ _ _ _ _
10 i _ _ _ r _ _ _ _
11 s _ _ _ _ _ _
  p _ _ _

2 ⭐ Look at the words in Exercise 1. How many are compound nouns? _____

3 ⭐ Write a place from Exercise 1.

1 I went there when I fell off my bike. ___hospital___

2 It was cold in there but we wore gloves and it was fun! _____

3 We went there to buy some clothes and presents.
_____

4 I went there to send a letter. _____

4 ⭐⭐ Complete the text with the places from Exercise 1.

My friend Edie lives in a small village. She always goes to the city to buy her clothes because there isn't a ¹shopping centre in her village. There's a library with lots of good books, and a ² _____ to send letters, but nothing else. There isn't a ³ _____ to watch films! I live in a big town and there's everything we need. I go to the ⁴ _____ to play tennis and take swimming classes at the ⁵ _____ . In December, I love ice skating at the ⁶ _____ and going bowling at the ⁷ _____ . My town has also got a ⁸ _____ – I was there last year when I broke my arm! But my favourite place is in the centre of town – it's an ⁹ _____ with lots of fish. My dad takes me there sometimes and leaves the car in a big ¹⁰ _____ . After that, I usually go skateboarding in a cool ¹¹ _____ nearby.

Explore it! 🖱

Guess the correct answer.
The first bowling alley opened in …
a London in 1889.   b New York in 1840.

Find another interesting fact about a place from Exercise 1 in your country. Then send a question in an email to a classmate or ask them it in the next class.

READING

An online travel article

1 ⭐ Look at the photos and read the article. Which photo (1–3) is the article not about? _____

2 ⭐⭐ Read the article and <u>underline</u> these words. Check their meaning in a dictionary and then complete the sentences.

> believe   belong   case
> ~~scuba diving~~   social media

1 I love swimming, but I prefer *scuba diving* underwater.

2 Matt's got a blog and shares his videos on _____ .

3 I can't _____ it! Our birthdays are on the same day!

4 Keep the camera safe. Put it in its _____ .

5 This cap isn't mine. Does it _____ to you?

3 ⭐⭐ Read the article again. Put the events in the correct order (1–8).

a Serina saw the photos on social media. ☐

b Serina went scuba diving. [1]

c The teacher put a message on social media. ☐

d The teacher looked at the photos on the camera. ☐

e Some schoolchildren found a camera on the beach. ☐

f Serina lost her camera. ☐

g The children and their teacher took the camera back to school. ☐

h Thousands of people shared the message. ☐

4 ⭐⭐⭐ Imagine you are Serina. Write a 'Thank you' message to Mr Park Lee and his class. Write at least four sentences.

Dear Mr Park Lee and students … _____

_____

_____

_____

Lost under the sea

In March 2018, a class from Mount Elementary School in Su'ao, Taiwan, went to clean the beach. They found a camera in an underwater case. They didn't know it was a camera at first because the case had things from the sea all over it. They showed their teacher, Mr Park Lee. He opened the case. Inside was a digital camera, and no sea water!

The class took the camera back to school. Everyone had questions: Did it work? Were there any photos in it? Did it belong to someone from Su'ao? Could they find him or her? The camera worked! Mr Park Lee looked at the photos. They showed fish and people underwater, and streets in Japan. Mr Lee put some photos with a message in Chinese and Japanese on social media. He asked people to share the message with their friends. In the next 24 hours, thousands of people saw the message. One of them was Serina Tsubakihara, a Japanese student. She couldn't believe it – they were her photos!

Serina went scuba diving near Okinawa, in Japan, in September 2015. She lost her camera there. It was in the sea for more than two years and travelled 250 kilometres to Taiwan!

LANGUAGE IN ACTION
Past simple: questions

1 ⭐ **Match questions 1–5 with answers a–e.**

1 Did Sami find his hat? [c]
2 Did the students go to the bowling alley? [ ]
3 Did you and Dana finish your project? [ ]
4 Did the ice rink close at six o'clock? [ ]
5 Did Rosa go to the cinema? [ ]

a Yes, we did.
b No, she didn't.
c Yes, he did.
d Yes, it did.
e No, they didn't.

2 ⭐ **Answer the questions for you. Tick (✓) the correct column.**

Yesterday, did you …	Yes, I did.	No, I didn't.
… have a big breakfast?		
… do any sport?		
… go to the cinema?		
… visit a family member?		
… hang out with friends after school?		

3 ⭐⭐ **Write the words in the correct order to make past simple questions.**

1 Alex / to / post office / Did / go / the / ?
Did Alex go to the post office?

2 buy / a / Clara / bag / new / Did / ?

3 Did / time / they / good / have / a / ?

4 aquarium / the / Did / enjoy / you / ?

5 your / Did / to / parents / walk / town / ?

4 ⭐⭐ **Write past simple questions. Do you know the answers?**

1 Shakespeare / write *Romeo and Juliet* / ?
Did Shakespeare write Romeo and Juliet?

2 Marie Curie / win a Nobel Prize / ?

3 Picasso / paint the *Mona Lisa* / ?

4 Columbus / discover Australia / ?

5 Emma Watson / sing in the film *Frozen* / ?

5 ⭐⭐⭐ **Complete the conversation with past simple questions. Use the words in brackets and the <u>underlined</u> verbs.**

MUM	Hi, there! ¹*Did you have a good match*? (you / good match)
RAHEEM	No, we <u>had</u> a terrible match.
MUM	Oh, no! ² _____? (your team)
RAHEEM	Yes. We <u>lost</u> 5–3.
MUM	³ _____? (you / a goal)
RAHEEM	No, I didn't <u>score</u> this time.
MUM	What about Henrik? ⁴ _____? (he)
RAHEEM	No, he didn't <u>play</u>. He fell off his skateboard the other day.
MUM	Oh, dear. ⁵ _____? (he / anything)
RAHEEM	Luckily he didn't <u>break</u> his leg. He just hurt it.
MUM	Good! ⁶ _____ after the match? (you / a snack)
RAHEEM	Yes, I <u>had</u> some chocolate. That was the best part!

VOCABULARY AND LISTENING
Personal possessions

1 ⭐ **Complete the definitions with the words in the box.**

> bus pass   camera   ~~headphones~~   ID card
> keys   money   passport   phone
> portable charger

We use …

1   _headphones_   to listen to music.
2   our _____ and _____ to show who we are.
3   _____ to buy things.
4   _____ to open a door.
5   a _____ to travel on public transport.
6   a _____ to text or talk to someone.
7   a _____ to take photos or make videos.
8   a _____ to keep our phone, tablet or laptop working.

2 ⭐⭐ **Complete the text with words from Exercise 1.**

| News | **Blog** | Lifestyle | [_____] 🔍 |

I had a bad day on Tuesday. I couldn't take the bus home because I couldn't find my ¹ _bus pass_ . Then I couldn't get into our flat because I didn't have my ² _____ . I used my ³ _____ to text my mum, but she was at the doctor's! I went to the library to do some homework on my laptop, but it had no battery and the ⁴ _____ was at home. I had some ⁵ _____ in my pocket, so I bought a drink at the café.
My sister loses things, too. Last July, she lost her ⁶ _____ on holiday and couldn't take any photos. Then she left her ⁷ _____ on a bus, so she couldn't listen to music on her phone. What a family!

A radio interview

🎧 **3** ⭐ **Look at the photos and answer the questions with your own ideas. Then listen and check your answers.**
8.01

1   What did Sabina lose? _____
2   Where did she find it / them? _____

🎧 **4** ⭐⭐ **Listen again. <u>Underline</u> and correct one mistake in each sentence.**
8.01

1   The tickets <u>weren't</u> Sabina's birthday present.
    _____were_____
2   Sabina asked her mum for help.
    _____
3   Sabina's friend put the envelope in the bin.
    _____
4   Sabina's CD wasn't in her room.
    _____
5   She didn't go to the concert. _____

🎧 **5** ⭐⭐ **Listen again and complete the sentences.**
8.01

1   The radio programme today is about
    _____ .
2   Sabina's best friend never _____ .
3   The questions helped Sabina _____ .

LANGUAGE IN ACTION
Past simple: *Wh-* questions

1 ⭐ Complete the questions with the question words in the box.

How much   What   When   ~~Where~~   Who

1 A: _____Where_____ did you buy your new headphones?   B: Round the corner.
2 A: _____ did they cost?   B: About €20.
3 A: _____ did you do last weekend?   B: I went to the cinema.
4 A: _____ did you go with?   B: My cousin.
5 A: _____ did you get that camera?   B: Last week, for my birthday.

2 ⭐⭐ Write past simple questions. Then match them with answers a–e.

1 What / you / do / last night?   ☐ e
   What did you do last night?

2 How / you / get / to school / today?   ☐
_____

3 Who / you / sit / with in class / yesterday?   ☐
_____

4 Where / you / go / last weekend?   ☐
_____

5 What time / get up / on Sunday?   ☐
_____

a My best friend.
b Really late! At 11 o'clock!
c I caught the bus.
d I went to the aquarium with my friends.
e ~~I watched TV and read a book.~~

3 ⭐⭐⭐ Complete the conversation with questions in the past simple. Use the answers to help you.

ANA   Hey! I went to a baseball match in Chicago.
ROB   Wow! When ¹_____did you go_____?
ANA   I went last weekend, on Saturday.
ROB   Who ²_____?
ANA   I went with my family and my American cousin, Martin
ROB   Who ³_____?
ANA   I sat with Martin. He told me everything about the game.

4 ⭐⭐⭐ Think about an interesting event you went to. Write the questions. Then answer them.

1 where / go?   *Where did you go?*
2 when / go?   _____
3 who / go with?   _____
4 how / feel?   _____

I went … _____
_____
_____

ROB   What ⁴_____?
ANA   I ate a big burger!
ROB   How ⁵_____?
ANA   We went home by bus.
ROB   What time ⁶_____?
ANA   I can't remember, but I know we got home really late!

WRITING
A blog post

1 ⭐ **Read the blog post. What problem started Bruno's bad day? (Circle) the correct answer.**

a His camera didn't work.

b His sister's camera didn't work.

c His parents' car didn't work.

● ● ● ●

HOME   **ABOUT ME**   ARCHIVE   FOLLOW

BRUNO'S BIG BLOG

A bad day at the weekend

1 Last Saturday it was my sister's birthday. We gave her a camera, but it didn't work. My mum and dad decided to go to the shopping centre to change it, so we all got ready.

2 When we got into the car, it didn't work, so we decided to take the bus. But it got worse! It started raining so we arrived wet and cold at the shop. Tragic. 😨

3 At the shop, the shop assistant asked for the receipt to change the camera, and guess what? My parents didn't have it … so my dad went back home to get it. After an hour, he came back and my sister got her new camera.

4 It was lunchtime, and we were really hungry, so we had lunch in the shopping centre. But when my parents wanted to pay, they couldn't find their wallets … they were at home! 😩

5 When did you have a bad day at the weekend? What happened? Tell me!

2 ⭐⭐ **Read the blog again. Put the events in the correct order (1–5).**

a Bruno's dad went back home. ☐

b They needed a receipt for the camera. ☐

c They took the bus to the shopping centre. ☐

d The family car didn't work. ☐ `1`

e Bruno's parents couldn't pay for lunch. ☐

3 ⭐⭐ **Join the sentences with so.**

1 It was my sister's birthday. We bought her a phone.

It was my sister's birthday, so we bought her a phone.

2 The phone didn't work. We decided to change it.

_____

3 My dad showed the receipt. My sister got her new phone.

_____

4 My parents couldn't find their wallets. They couldn't pay for lunch.

_____

4 **Read the blog post again. Match topics a–e with paragraphs 1–5.**

a what happened next ☐

b what day it was and how it started ☐

c what happened later ☐

d sign off and ask questions ☐

e the end of the bad day ☐

Write a blog post about a bad day at the weekend.

PLAN

5 ⭐⭐ **Make notes about your bad day. Think about the answers to these questions.**

> When did the bad day start?
> What problems did you and your family / friends have?
> When and where did each problem happen?
> What did you do? What did the other people do?
> How did you feel?

6 Decide what information to include in each paragraph. Use the information in Exercise 4 to help you.

WRITE

7 ⭐⭐⭐ **Write your blog post. Remember to include four paragraphs, the past simple for the questions at the end and the expressions from the *Useful language* box (see Student's Book, p101).**

CHECK

8 Do you …
- use a title for your blog post?
- use so to join ideas and explain the results?
- say how you felt on your bad day?

VOCABULARY

1 Where did Tim go last week? Match the sentences with the words in the box. There are four extra words.

> aquarium   bowling alley   car park
> cinema   hospital   ice rink
> post office   shopping centre
> skate park   sports centre   swimming pool

1 He posted a letter for his grandma.

_____

2 He watched a basketball match. _____

3 He visited his sick uncle. _____

4 He watched an amazing film. _____

5 He bought a new pair of jeans. _____

6 He saw lots of dolphins! _____

7 He dived into the water. _____

2 Which four places from Exercise 1 didn't Tim go to?

_____   _____

_____   _____

3 Complete the sentences with the words in the box.

> camera   concert tickets   headphones
> keys   money   passport   phone   tablet

1 I haven't got any _____ to buy a drink.

2 You need your _____ to travel to a different country.

3 These _____ don't work. I can't hear anything!

4 These days, everyone's got a _____ to text and call people.

5 It's easy to use a _____ . You just touch the screen and it works!

6 Let's buy _____ to see Sia.

7 Héctor doesn't use his phone to take photos. He uses his _____ .

8 Where are the _____ to open the door?

LANGUAGE IN ACTION

4 Complete the dialogue with the past simple questions and short answers. Use the verbs in brackets.

ARINA	[1]_____ you _____ (go) to the bowling alley yesterday, Max?
MAX	Yes, I [2]_____ .
ARINA	[3]_____ you _____ (meet) Olga there?
MAX	No, I [4]_____ . I was with Alex and Elena.
ARINA	Cool! And [5]_____ you _____ (have) a good time?
MAX	No, we [6]_____ . Alex dropped the bowling ball on his foot!
ARINA	Oh, dear! Poor Alex! [7]_____ his parents _____ (take) him to hospital?
MAX	Yes, they [8]_____ .
ARINA	Was his foot OK? [9]_____ he _____ (break) it?
MAX	No, he [10]_____ . He was very lucky!

5 Write past simple questions.

1 What / you / do / last night?

2 How / your dad / get to work / this morning?

3 What time / you / arrive home / after school?

4 Who / you / see / yesterday?

5 Where / you / go / last weekend?

6 How / you / feel / after the exam?

CUMULATIVE LANGUAGE

6 Complete the conversation with the missing words. (Circle) the correct options.

BRENDA Hi, Theo. Where ¹_____ go yesterday?

THEO I ²_____ to the ice rink to watch my brother.

BRENDA ³_____ go ice skating, too?

THEO No! I don't ⁴_____ ice skating. I think it's dangerous!

BRENDA Yes, me too! The first time I ⁵_____ it I nearly ⁶_____ my leg!

THEO The other problem is that ⁷_____ usually a lot of people on the ice.

BRENDA Yes, you're right! ⁸_____ does your brother go?

THEO He ⁹_____ every week for about three hours. He says he wants to be the ¹⁰_____ ice skater in town!

BRENDA ¹¹_____ you at the ice rink all day yesterday?

THEO Yes, but he ¹²_____ me for dinner afterwards!

1	a do you	b did you	c you did
2	a go	b went	c goes
3	a Did you	b You	c Were you
4	a like	b likes	c liked
5	a try	b tries	c tried
6	a broke	b break	c breaks
7	a there is	b there are	c there were
8	a How often	b How many	c How
9	a practise	b practises	c practised
10	a good	b better	c best
11	a Did	b Was	c Were
12	a take	b took	c takes

VOCABULARY
Outdoor life

1 ⭐ Look at the pictures. Complete the activities with the words and phrases in the box.

> a compass   a fire   a map   a shelter
> fish   ~~food and water~~   fruit
> over a campfire   plants   wood

1 find _food and water_

2 cook _____

3 pick _____

4 identify _____

5 light _____

6 catch _____

7 collect _____

8 build _____

9 use _____

10 read _____

2 ⭐⭐ Match the sentences with activities from Exercise 1.

a You do this before nighttime. You sleep there. ⟨8⟩

b You need to do this before you light a fire. ☐

c You need to find trees with apples, pears, etc. to do this. ☐

d You need to do this to see different places and where they are. ☐

e You do this to know which way to go. ☐

f You do this to keep warm and to cook. ☐

g You do this when you are hungry or thirsty. ☐

3 ⭐⭐ Complete the text with the correct form of the verbs from Exercise 1.

> I often go to the mountains with my family. When we get there, some of us ¹ _collect_ wood for the fire and others ² _____ a shelter. Next, we all go to ³ _____ water and ⁴ _____ fish for lunch. My dad always ⁵ _____ the fish over a campfire. It can take a long time to ⁶ _____ the fire if the wood is wet. In the afternoon, we go for a walk to ⁷ _____ plants. I write their names in my notebook. We sometimes ⁸ _____ fruit, too. We ⁹ _____ a compass in the mountains because it's easy to get lost!

4 ⭐⭐⭐ Write about one or more outdoor activities that you do in the holidays. Look at Exercise 3 to help you.

_____

_____

Explore it!

Guess the correct answer.

In this country, students have the longest school summer holidays in Europe. They get 13 weeks! Which country is it?

a Italy   b Germany   c Portugal

Find an interesting fact about how people spend their free time in your country. Then send a question in an email to a classmate or ask them it in the next class.

READING
A leaflet

ADVENTURE TRIPS

[FI]ND AN ADVENTURE TRIP FOR YOU THIS SUMMER!

[Yo]u'll learn new things and have lots of fun!
[Jo]in us on one of our three Adventure Trips.
[R]ead and choose the best one for you!

1. WHITE WATER KAYAKING TRIP (THREE DAYS)

Day 1: Meet your instructors and practise on white water.

Day 2: Learn how to use a compass and choose the best part of the river for your kayak.

Day 3: Follow the fast water and show your instructors how good you are!

We'll also teach you to build a shelter and help you collect wood for a campfire.

2. MOUNTAIN CLIMBING TRIP (FIVE DAYS)

Days 1–2: Walk five kilometres in the mountains each day with your guide. Learn how to identify plants and pick the right fruit to eat!

Days 3–5: Spend three days mountain climbing. Learn how to read a map and help each other.

You won't get much time to sit down! But you'll become the best mountain climber!

3. WATER AND COUNTRYSIDE TRIP (SIX DAYS)

Day 1: Learn how to catch fish in the river and then cook them over a campfire!

Days 2–3: Travel along the river in a canoe and work as a team.

Days 4–6: Leave the water to go horse riding in the countryside with your guides!

You won't be bored on this trip. We'll play fun games and you'll make good friends!

WHAT ARE YOU WAITING FOR?
CHOOSE THE BEST ADVENTURE TRIP FOR YOU!

You'll learn new sports and skills, meet new people and have a great time!

For more information and booking details, visit our website.

We'll give you breakfast and lunch, but sometimes … you'll need to find your own dinner!

---

1 ☆ **Read the leaflet. Then complete the sentences with the phrases in the box.**

> White water kayaking   Mountain climbing
> Water and countryside

1 You can learn how to read a map and identify plants on the _____ trip.

2 You can learn how to cook your own food over a campfire on the _____ trip.

3 You can learn how to use a compass on the _____ trip.

2 ☆☆ **Read the leaflet again and <u>underline</u> these words. Then check their meaning in a dictionary and complete the sentences.**

> white water   ~~river~~   follow   guides   spend

1 There are lots of fish in that ___river___ .

2 The water in a river that moves very quickly is called _____ .

3 Our mountain _____ showed us some good places to climb.

4 Don't walk alone in the forest. Always _____ the instructor.

5 I need to _____ more time learning how to build a shelter!

3 ☆☆☆ **Answer the questions.**

1 On Trip 1, who do you meet on Day 1?
___your instructors___

2 On which day do you use a compass?
_____

3 On Trip 2, how far do you walk on day one?
_____

4 What things can you learn on Trip 2?
_____

5 On Trip 3, when do you do water activities?
_____

4 ☆☆☆ **Answer the questions with your own ideas.**

1 Which trip is the most exciting? Why?
_____

2 Which trip is the most difficult? Why?
_____

LANGUAGE IN ACTION
Future with *will/won't*

1 ⭐ (Circle) the correct options.

1 The climbing trip *be* / (*will be*) good fun. It *not will* / *won't* be boring.

2 We *won't* / *not will* make our own lunch. The instructors *make will* / *will make* it.

3 A: *Will you* / *You will* go on the kayaking trip?
  B: Yes, *I'll* / *I will*.

4 A: *Will* / *Will not* the instructors make dinner for you?
  B: No, they *not will* / *won't*.

2 ⭐⭐ Write sentences with *I'll* or *I won't*.

1 (✓) learn how to catch fish
  I'll learn how to catch fish.

2 (✗) get bored
  _____

3 (✓) go in a canoe
  _____

4 (✗) stay for two weeks
  _____

5 (✓) walk six kilometres
  _____

6 (✓) cook food over a campfire
  _____

3 ⭐⭐ Complete the email with the correct form of *will* and the verbs in brackets.

● ● ●

Hi Victoria,

I got back a few hours ago from my family camping trip. It was OK, but my sister says she ¹ _won't go_ (not go) again. She also ² _____ (not sleep) in a shelter again! She says she ³ _____ (go) with her friends on a beach holiday because it ⁴ _____ (be) sunny and they ⁵ _____ (not do) anything all day – just sleep and swim! She's 18 now, so I guess we ⁶ _____ (not be) together next summer. I ⁷ _____ (miss) her! How was your holiday?

4 ⭐⭐ Write the words in the correct order to make questions. Then answer the questions for you in your notebook.

1 with your family / Will / this year / you / go on holiday / ?
  Will you go on holiday with your family this year?

2 you / Will / see / at the weekend / your best friend / ?
  _____

3 tomorrow / will / you / do / What / ?
  _____

4 this summer / go / you / Where / will / ?
  _____

5 will / you / Who / next week / see / ?
  _____

6 go shopping / you / Will / tomorrow / ?
  _____

5 ⭐⭐⭐ You are going on one of the adventure trips from the leaflet on p73. Make four predictions about it with *will/won't*.

I'll make new friends.

1 _____
2 _____
3 _____
4 _____

VOCABULARY AND LISTENING
Holidays

1 ☆ Complete the accommodation words in the spidergram with the missing vowels.

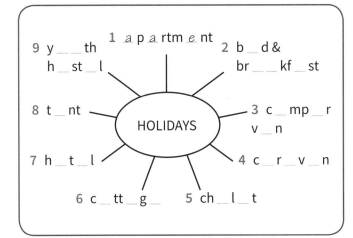

Spidergram – HOLIDAYS

- 1 a p a r tm e nt
- 2 b _ d & br _ _ kf _ st
- 3 c _ mp _ r v _ n
- 4 c _ r _ v _ n
- 5 ch _ l _ t
- 6 c _ tt _ g _
- 7 h _ t _ l
- 8 t _ nt
- 9 y _ _ th h _ st _ l

2 ☆☆ Complete the text with words from Exercise 1.

My family and I want to go on holiday, but everyone wants to stay in a different place! My dad wants to stay in a ¹h otel_____, but my mum prefers a ²b_____ & b_____. My brother loves moving from place to place, so he thinks a ³c_____ v_____ is perfect! My grandma wants a little house like a ⁴c_____, but my dad says that's very small. My aunt showed me a picture of an amazing city ⁵a_____. It looks great, but I want to stay in a ⁶y_____ h_____ – it's the best place to make friends!

A conversation

🎧 **3** 9.01 ☆ Listen to the conversation. Where will the girls spend their summer holidays? (Circle) the correct answer.

a in a cottage   b at home   c in the USA

🎧 **4** 9.01 ☆☆ Listen again. Match the phrases with the people in the box.

> aunt and uncle   Camila   ~~parents~~   Yana

1 on holiday in another country ___parents___
2 really good fun _____
3 at home with her parents in the summer

_____
4 invites her friend to do an outdoor activity

_____

🎧 **5** 9.01 ☆☆ Listen again and answer the questions.

1 How will Camila's parents travel around the USA?

_in a camper van_____

2 Who will be with Camila for two weeks?

_____

3 Whose parents have got a holiday cottage?

_____

4 What will the parents of Camila's friend do in July and August?

_____

5 Why does Camila ask her friend to stay with her?

_____

6 Why doesn't Camila's friend like camping?

_____

6 ☆☆☆ Your parents are going on holiday and you will stay at home with someone else from your family. Make a spidergram with positive/negative things about this.

LANGUAGE IN ACTION
Present continuous for future

1 ⭐ **Match 1–6 with a–f.**

1 My mum's working on Saturday. `c`
2 Are you watching the match tomorrow? ☐
3 Mario isn't playing tennis after school. ☐
4 Are your cousins arriving soon? ☐
5 We're going on a school trip tomorrow. ☐
6 How are you getting to the sports centre? ☐

a We're visiting a museum.
b My dad's driving me.
c ~~She's going to a meeting.~~
d He's going to the dentist.
e No, I'm not. I'm studying.
f Yes, they are. On Sunday.

2 ⭐⭐ **Write sentences with the present continuous.**

1 We / go / to the beach / at the weekend
   We're going to the beach at the weekend.
2 Debra / not have / a birthday party / this year
3 My grandparents / fly / to Italy / in August
4 You / have / lunch / at a restaurant / on Sunday / ?
5 We / not do / anything special / this weekend
6 How / she / get / to work / today / ?

3 ⭐⭐ **Complete the conversation with the present continuous form of the verbs in brackets.**

CARLA What ¹ *are you doing* (you / do) in the summer?

NICO In July I ² _____ (go) to a summer camp in the mountains.

CARLA That sounds fun! ³ _____ (you / sleep) in a tent?

NICO No, I ⁴ _____ (not camp). We ⁵ _____ (stay) in chalets.

CARLA What ⁶ _____ (your parents / do)?

NICO They ⁷ _____ (start) their holidays in August. They ⁸ _____ (meet) me at the summer camp and we ⁹ _____ (drive) across the country in a camper van.

be going to

4 ⭐ **Underline and correct one mistake in each sentence.**

1 We going to visit the water park.   *We're going*
2 Are you going see the new film? _____
3 I'm not go to buy a camera. _____
4 They're going living in the country. _____
5 Mia isn't to go swimming after school. _____
6 Leo going to learn to skateboard. _____

5 ⭐⭐⭐ **Write questions with the present continuous or be going to. Then write answers for you.**

1 What / do / this weekend? (present continuous)
   What are you doing this weekend?
2 What / do / tonight? (present continuous)
3 What TV programmes / watch / this week? (be going to)
4 How / celebrate / your birthday / this year? (be going to)

WRITING

An email

1 ⭐ **Read the email. How does Paige know Ava?**

_____

2 ⭐⭐ (Circle) **the correct prepositions (1–10) in the email.**

● ● ●

Hi Ava,

1 Thanks for your email. I'm really excited you're coming to stay with us in New Zealand ¹*on* / (*in*) January! 👏 We'll have a great time! You'll enjoy Mission Bay and seeing our friends from primary school again.

2 Here are the arrangements. ²*On* / *In* Friday, Mum and I are meeting you ³*at* / *on* the airport in Auckland. Then we're going to have a night ⁴*in* / *at* home and my dad's cooking. You're sleeping with me ⁵*in* / *at* my room. We can talk about your new life in Australia and compare our schools! 🙂

3 ⁶*In* / *On* Saturday, we're going to the beach. 🌞 It'll be hot, so we'll go swimming. Hayley, Lily and Ryan from our primary class are coming, too! ⁷*In* / *On* the evening, we're going to have dinner ⁸*on* / *at* my favourite restaurant. Then ⁹*on* / *at* Sunday, we're going to Te Urewera National Park for four days. We're staying ¹⁰*in* / *on* a nice chalet. There are beautiful lakes and birds. What do you think?

4 It'll be great to see you again! Is there anything you would like to do? Let me know!

See you soon, 👍

Paige xx

3 **Match topics a–d with paragraphs 1–4.**

a end the email ☐

b respond to your penfriend's last email ☐

c describe the first day ☐

d describe the weekend ☐

4 ⭐⭐ **Read the email again. Are the sentences _T_ (true) or _F_ (false)?**

1 Ava is travelling to Auckland by car. _____F_____

2 Ava and Paige are sleeping in the same room. _____

3 They're spending one day at the beach. _____

4 They're having dinner at home on Saturday evening. _____

5 At Te Urewera National Park, they're not staying in a hotel. _____

Write an email to a friend from primary school about plans for their visit.

PLAN

5 ⭐⭐ **Your friend from primary school now lives in another place and is coming to stay with you. Make notes about these things for your email:**

> your arrangements
> things you intend to do
> predictions about what will happen
> the place where you are meeting them.

6 ⭐⭐ **Decide what information to include in each paragraph. Use the information in Exercise 3 to help you.**

WRITE

7 ⭐⭐⭐ **Write your email. Remember to include four paragraphs, _will_, _going to_ and the present continuous for future, and expressions from the _Useful language_ box (see Student's Book, p113).**

CHECK

8 **Do you ...**

* include an arrangement and a prediction for the weekend and the week ahead?
* make predictions about what will or won't happen?
* tell your penfriend where you are going to meet them?

VOCABULARY

1 (Circle) the correct verb.

1 *catch* / *build* a shelter
2 *light* / *cook* a fire
3 *build* / *pick* fruit
4 *catch* / *light* fish

5 *use* / *cook* over a campfire
6 *collect* / *build* wood
7 *read* / *collect* a map
8 *build* / *identify* plants

2 Find nine words for accommodation in the word search. Then match them with sentences 1–9 below.

C	T	E	N	T	Y	B	E	G	F	B
A	B	C	L	H	O	C	I	J	N	E
M	C	H	O	I	U	E	O	G	C	D
P	A	A	M	K	T	G	U	B	T	&
E	I	L	E	M	H	O	T	E	L	B
R	T	E	Y	R	H	M	E	V	L	R
V	F	T	X	C	O	T	T	A	G	E
A	K	C	Z	W	S	N	A	S	A	A
N	A	P	A	R	T	M	E	N	T	K
J	O	G	U	X	E	Q	M	R	B	F
K	P	E	W	O	L	T	X	S	C	A
M	R	V	C	A	R	A	V	A	N	S
O	U	H	O	H	I	R	A	Y	S	T

1 This can be a problem in the rain. _____
2 A place where young people normally stay. _____
3 You can drive with your bed in this! _____
4 A small country house. _____
5 You need a car to move this. _____
6 You only stay here to sleep and eat in the morning. _____
7 This is in a building, often in a city. _____
8 An expensive one has got five stars. _____
9 A small house usually made of wood. _____

LANGUAGE IN ACTION

3 Complete the conversation with the correct form of *will* or *won't*. Use the verbs in brackets.

● ● ●

| Wall | Find friends | Chat |

IAN   1h ago
¹ _____ (we / sleep) in tents?

GUIDE   1h ago
No, you ² _____ (not sleep) in a tent. You ³ _____ (stay) in a chalet. Every night, we ⁴ _____ (cook) dinner over a campfire.

IAN   1h ago
Sounds fun. What activities ⁵ _____ (we / do)?

GUIDE   1h ago
You ⁶ _____ (go) walking and climbing in the mountains. We ⁷ _____ (teach) you how to read a map so you ⁸ _____ (not get) lost. It ⁹ _____ (be) fantastic. You ¹⁰ _____ (not forget) the experience, I'm sure!

4 Complete the email with the present continuous form of the verbs in brackets.

● ● ●

Hi Sonia,

What ¹ _____ (you / do) this summer? In July, my parents ² _____ (work), so Pau and I ³ _____ (not / plan) anything special. He ⁴ _____ (go) to a football camp and I ⁵ _____ (stay) with my grandparents. Then in August we ⁶ _____ (fly) to Croatia for a family holiday. My parents ⁷ _____ (rent) an apartment at the beach, and then we ⁸ _____ (drive) up to the mountains in a camper van. I'm very excited!

5 Write sentences about the pictures. Use the correct form of *be going to* and the phrases in the box.

> climb a mountain   get on a plane   go horse riding   play volleyball
> sleep in a tent   walk in the forest

1 He _____

2 She _____

3 He _____

4 She _____

5 They _____

6 They _____

CUMULATIVE LANGUAGE

6 Complete the text with the missing words. (Circle) the correct options.

I had ¹_____ amazing holiday of my life last year. ²_____ go? I went to Turkey on ³_____ adventure holiday! We built a shelter to sleep in and learned ⁴_____ new things, like how to catch fish and find fruit to eat in the forest. We did ⁵_____ sports, too. They were fun! I loved ⁶_____ kayaking but I ⁷_____ horse riding. It was frightening! I've got a lot of photos. Would you like to see ⁸_____?

This holiday was ⁹_____ than my holiday two years ago. Now I ¹⁰_____ lots of new friends. At the moment, we ¹¹_____ emails to each other to get together this year. I can't ¹²_____!

1	a the more	b most	c the most
2	a Where did I	b What I did	c When did I
3	a some	b a	c an
4	a much	b a lot	c a lot of
5	a an	b any	c some
6	a going	b go	c do
7	a wasn't enjoy	b didn't enjoy	c not enjoy
8	a them	b they	c it
9	a better	b the best	c good
10	a 's got	b got	c 've got
11	a writing	b 're writing	c write
12	a to wait	b wait	c waiting

EXAM TIPS: Reading skills

Reading Part 2: Multiple matching

In this part of the test you have to read three short texts about three different people.
They are all about the same topic. The title tells you what the topic is. There are seven questions.
They all start with: *Which person …?* The answer to each question is the name of one of the three people.
To answer the question you need to (circle) the correct answer, A, B or C.

Example:

	Tim	Tom	Ted
Which person did a lot of sport at school?	*A*	*B*	*C*

Exam guide: Multiple matching

- Start by reading the title of the text so you know what the topic is.

- Read all the questions carefully and <u>underline</u> the important words. This helps when you look for the same information in the texts.

  Example:

  Which person did <u>a lot of sport</u> at <u>school</u>?

- Now read the three texts for the first time without stopping. Maybe you see information similar to the questions, but read to the end.

- Now read the first question again. Then look at the texts to find which person says this. Maybe you remember something from one of the texts, so go to that text first to check. If not, just read from the beginning until you find what you need.

- When you find the correct answer, <u>underline</u> the words in the text with the same meaning as the question. Write the number of the question next to the part you <u>underlined</u>. Then circle your answer, A, B or C.

  Example:

  When I was a teenager I <u>was in the school hockey, athletics and swimming teams.</u>

- Then read the next question and do the same until you finish.
- You don't lose points for a wrong answer, so always (circle) a letter, even if you're not sure.

REMEMBER!

When you look for the answer, remember that the words in the question are probably different from the words in the text, but the meaning is the same. So if you see a word in the text that is the same as a word in the question, it is not automatically the correct answer.

Example:

I did a lot of sport after school when I was younger.

This is **NOT** the correct answer to the example question, because the meaning is different from the question.

Reading Part 2 practice: Multiple matching

1 <u>Underline</u> the most important words in these questions.

0 Which person does <u>a lot of sport</u> at the <u>weekend</u>?

Which person

1 loves trying new activities after school?

2 has got a lot of online friends?

3 reads science and nature magazines on the internet?

4 wants to study art or drama at school next year?

5 hasn't got any aunts, uncles or cousins?

6 doesn't like living in a big city?

> **Tip!**
> Underlining the most important words in the questions helps you to remember the information you need to find in the text.

2 Match words 1–9 with their opposites in the box.

> after   boring   difficult   evening   finish   good   hate   late   short   ~~small~~

0 big   ___small___

1 easy   _____

2 early   _____

3 love   _____

4 long   _____

5 start   _____

6 before   _____

7 morning   _____

8 fun   _____

9 bad   _____

> **Tip!**
> When reading the text, look for words or phrases which are opposites (often with a negative verb) or synonyms of the words in the question.

3 Read the text and match the words in **bold** with the synonyms 1–9.

One place in my **road** that's very popular with **young people** is the skate park. Some of my friends spend all their **leisure time** there. There is also a **big** sports centre near me, with some good **courses**, like swimming and dancing. **Many** of my friends **tell me** they would like to go there too, but the **price** is too high. I **travel** to a cheaper gym but it's not very near my house and so it's **difficult** to get to.

0 street   ___road___

1 a lot   _____

2 large   _____

3 say   _____

4 free time   _____

5 teenagers   _____

6 hard   _____

7 go   _____

8 cost   _____

9 classes   _____

4 Choose the option, A or B, which has the same meaning as the question.

0 Which person has a lot of homework to do?

   (A) I spend about two hours every night on school work.

   B In my school the teachers don't usually give us much homework.

1 Which person isn't happy about their hair colour?

   A I've got red hair but I don't mind. It's the same as Ed Sheeran's!

   B Everyone in my family has got blonde hair. It's boring. I want to be different.

2 Which person reads information about science on the internet?

   A There is so much interesting stuff to read online these days, especially science articles.

   B I love reading my dad's science magazines. He buys them every month.

3 Which person doesn't mind getting up early in the morning?

   A I have to get up at seven so I'm not late for school, but that isn't a problem.

   B I'm glad when it's Saturday and I can get up late.

4 Which person thinks living in the country is boring?

   A People say that the country is boring but I think there's lots to do.

   B I'm happy I live in the city. I'm sure it's more exciting than being in a village.

EXAM TIPS: Writing skills

Writing Part 6: Writing a short email or note

In this part of the test, you have to write a short email or note of 25 words or more. Under the instructions there is a space to write the text.

The instructions in the test tell you exactly what you need to do.

Example:

*You want to **go to the cinema** with **your friend** Jan on **Saturday**. Write an email to Jan.*

The instructions also explain three things you need to include in the text. For example:

In the email:
- **ask** Jan to **go to the cinema** with you
- say **what film** you want to see
- say **where** you can **meet**.

> ### Exam guide: Writing a short email or note
>
> - It is important to include all the points from the instructions in the text. It is also better to keep them in the same order as in the instructions.
>
> - The text needs
>   - an opening sentence
>   - three sentences, one for each point
>   - a sentence to close (for example a question asking your friend's opinion)
>   - (in an email) your name at the end.
>
> - When you finish, read the text again and count the number of words. If you have included all the information from the plan above, the text should be at least 25 words. If it's more, that's OK. If you haven't written 25 words, go back and check that you have included all the points and the opening and the closing sentences.

Writing Part 7: Writing a short story

In this part of the test, you have to write a short story of 35 words or more. To help you there are three pictures. You write the story they show. Under the pictures there is a space to write your story.

> ### Exam guide: Writing a short story
>
> - Don't start writing immediately. Look at the pictures for a minute and decide what the story is about. A good way to plan a story is to think about *Who? Where? When?* and *What?*
>
> - Give any people in the picture a name. Then write any useful vocabulary you want to use (nouns, verbs, adjectives, etc.) next to each picture.
>
> - Decide how to start (e.g. *One day/Yesterday*). Use the past tense when you write your story.
>
> - When you finish writing, count the words. You need to write at least 35 words.

REMEMBER!

You will be given a piece of paper to make notes. Use it to plan your writing.

Writing Parts 6 & 7 practice: An email or note; a short story

1 Match the phrases from a text message with the right category A–C.

> **Tip!**
> For this part of the test, try to use different phrases for inviting and suggesting ideas.

> A opening   B inviting or suggesting   C closing phrase

0 I'd like to see the new X-men film. __B__

1 What do you think? _____
2 Do you want to go swimming this afternoon? _____
3 Let me know soon. _____
4 Hey _____

5 Shall we meet at the bus stop at seven? _____
6 Hi Jan _____
7 We can try the new pool. _____
8 How about going to the cinema on Saturday? _____

2 Order the words to make sentences from an email.

0 cheap / to / a / go / restaurant / Let's / . Let's go to a cheap restaurant.

1 want / in / Do / holidays / to / you / meet / the / ?

_____

2 for / Why / days / we / don't / go / a few / camping / ?

_____

3 what / know / Let / you / me / think / .

_____

4 Tania / Hi / ,

_____

5 climbing / I'd / go / again / to / like / .

_____

6 my / can / tent / take / We / brother's / .

_____

3 Separate the text into words and sentences. Then rewrite the email with the correct format and punctuation in your notebook.

> **Tip!**
> Always check your writing for spelling or punctuation.

heyjosedoyouwanttohangouttogetheronsaturdaywecangotothe
newshoppingcentreshallicometoyourhouseatfourletmeknowsoonpepe

Hey Jose,

4 Correct the spelling of these words.

0 swiming ___swimming___

1 shoping _____
2 wich _____
3 tenis _____

4 Wenesday _____
5 tomorow _____
6 bycicle _____

7 diferent _____
8 scool _____
9 begining _____

5 Put the words in the box in the correct place in the story.

> **Tip!**
> Use time words like *yesterday*, *after* or *then* to make the order of events clear. Use words like *but* and *so* to show how the events connect.

> After   but   so   Then   ~~Yesterday~~

0 ___Yesterday___ Annie had a technology presentation at school, *1* _____ she got up late. *2* _____ she got to school, she saw her notes weren't in her bag. They were important, *3* _____ she phoned her dad and asked him to look for them. He found them in her room. *4* _____ he brought her notes to school. She was very happy.

EXAM TIPS: Listening skills

Listening Part 4: Three-option multiple choice

In this part of the test you listen to five short texts. You always hear the text twice. Each text is about something different, and the question usually explains who is speaking, who they are speaking to and what they are talking about.

Example:

*You will hear **two friends** talking about **their plans for the weekend**.*

You then have to answer a question about each text, with three options, A, B and C.

Example:

*You will hear two friends talking about their plans for the weekend. **What do they both plan to do?***

A *They are **both going** to a **basketball match**.*

B *They are **both visiting** their **grandparents**.*

C *They are **both going shopping** with **friends**.*

You can write your answers on the question paper. At the end of the test, you will have six minutes to put all your answers on a separate answer sheet.

Exam guide: Three-option multiple choice

- You have time before you listen to read the questions. Read them carefully because they tell you what you need to listen for.

- <u>Underline</u> the important words in the question. In the example the most important word in the question is **both**.

  Example:

  A *They are <u>both</u> going to a basketball match.*

  B *They are <u>both</u> visiting their grandparents.*

  C *They are <u>both</u> going shopping with friends.*

- When you listen the first time, try and decide what the correct answer is and circle A, B or C. If you're not sure, don't worry. The second time you listen you can check your first answer or decide for the first time.

- Sometimes the first time you listen you hear that one answer is definitely wrong. Cross it out. Then the second time you listen, just focus on the other two possible answers.

- Always give an answer, even if you don't know which one is correct. You don't lose points for a wrong answer.

- When you have heard one text twice, don't spend a lot of time thinking about it. Focus on the next listening text when it starts.

REMEMBER!

You will usually hear the people talk about all the possible answers in some way but this is a 'trap'. Only one answer is correct.

To avoid 'traps', listen carefully to every word. You will hear negative verbs (for example: *I'm not visiting my grandparents this weekend*) or things which are similar but not the same as the correct answer (for example: *I'm going shopping with my sister on Saturday*).

Listening Part 4 practice: Three-option multiple choice

🎧 **1** **Listen to the sentences. Write Y (yes) if they are positive or N (no) if they are negative.**
E.01
     1 _____   2 _____   3 _____   4 _____   5 _____   6 _____

🎧 **2** **Is the meaning of the sentences you hear the same as sentences 1–6? Write Y (yes) or N (no).**
E.02
     1 I decided not to buy the shirt because I didn't like the colour. _____

     2 It takes Martin a quarter of an hour to walk home. _____

     3 It was sunny yesterday. _____

     4 Martin is flying to Spain on holiday. _____

     5 Paula's sister has got dark hair. _____

     6 The teacher tells Eric to do his homework again. _____

🎧 **3** **Read sentences 1–6. Then listen and correct the information that is different.**
E.03
     1 Alex went to Scotland by coach last year. _____

     2 Laia is going to stay in a hotel with her grandparents. _____

     3 Donna usually goes to the bowling alley at the weekend. _____

     4 Harry lost his bus pass yesterday. _____

     5 Last week Megan saw a programme about bears on TV. _____

     6 Tom has got a basketball match on Saturday morning. _____

🎧 **4** **Listen and choose the correct option, A or B. You will hear each text twice.**
E.04
     1 The teacher has got a problem with Sarah's homework because

       A she made a lot of mistakes.

       B she did the wrong page.

     2 What's the weather like today?

       A It's cold and wet.

       B It's cloudy and warm.

     3 What did Corrin and Vanessa do today?

       A They went out for a meal.

       B They went out with school friends.

     4 How did Nico get home after the concert?

       A He caught the last bus.

       B His friend's dad gave him a lift.

     5 What did Ollie buy at the shopping centre?

       A a new sports bag

       B some new joggers

     6 What does Chloe's mother want her to do?

       A go shopping

       B tidy her room

Subject pronouns

Singular	Plural
I	we
you	you
he / she / it	they

- We use a subject pronoun before a verb.
  She is Brazilian. (NOT ~~Is Brazilian~~.)
- The singular and plural form of **you** is the same.

Possessive adjectives

Singular	Plural
my	our
your	your
his / her / its	their

- We use possessive adjectives to show that something belongs to somebody. We always use possessive adjectives with a noun.
  Our house is big.   *Their school is fun.*

Verb *be*

Affirmative	Negative
I'm Turkish.	I'm not Turkish.
You're Turkish	You aren't Turkish.
He's / She's / It's Turkish.	He / She / It isn't Turkish.
We're Turkish.	We aren't Turkish.
You're Turkish.	You aren't Turkish.
They're Turkish.	They aren't Turkish.

Question	Short answer	
	Affirmative	Negative
Am I Turkish?	Yes, I am.	No, I'm not.
Are you Turkish?	Yes, you are.	No, you aren't.
Is he / she / it Turkish?	Yes, he / she / it is.	No, he / she / it isn't.
Are we Turkish?	Yes, we are.	No we aren't.
Are you Turkish?	Yes, you are.	No, you aren't.
Are they Turkish?	Yes, they are.	No, they aren't.

- We use **be** to identify or describe something.
  They're red.   *He's Spanish.*   *It's good.*
- We usually use contractions in conversation.
  We're from Canada.   *She's ten.*

- We change the word order in questions; we put **be** before the subject.
  Is David OK?   *Are you from London?*
  (NOT ~~You are from London?~~)
- We usually reply with short answers.
  A: *Is it blue?* **B:** *Yes, it is.*   **A:** *Is it red?* **B:** *No, it isn't.*

Question words

- We use **what** to ask for information.
  What is your favourite colour?
- We use **where** to ask about places.
  Where are you from?
- We use **when** to ask about time.
  When is your birthday?
- We use **how old** to ask about age.
  How old is your father?
- We use **who** to ask about people.
  Who is your best friend?

whose + possessive pronouns

Whose book is this?	Singular	Plural
	It's mine.	It's ours.
	It's yours.	It's yours.
	It's his / hers.	It's theirs.

- **whose** asks about possession or ownership.
- We often use possessive pronouns to answer **whose** questions. They help us to avoid repeating information.
  Whose pencil is this? It's mine. (NOT ~~It's my pencil.~~)
  We don't use **its** as a possessive pronoun.
  Whose book is this? (NOT ~~It's its.~~)
- We use **this** (singular) and **these** (plural) to talk about things that are near.
  This is my pencil.   *These are my books.*
- We use **that** (singular) and **those** (plural) to talk about things that are not near.
  That is my schoolbag.   *Those are my pens.*

Imperatives

Affirmative	Negative
Stand up!	Don't stand up!
Open the book!	Don't open the book!

- We use the imperative to give orders or instructions.
  Come here, please.
- We use **don't** to form the negative.
  Don't write in your textbook.

LANGUAGE PRACTICE

Subject pronouns and possessive adjectives

1 Complete the sentences with the correct subject pronouns and possessive adjectives.

1 My best friend Maria is from Paris. ___She___ 's French. ___Her___ house is very big!

2 My name's Pablo. _____ 'm from Ecuador. I'm in _____ classroom.

3 Berat and Ahmet are Turkish– _____ 're from Istanbul. These are _____ books.

4 My English teacher is John. _____ 's from London. _____ classes are fun!

5 Susie, _____ 're my friend! Today is _____ birthday! Happy birthday!

Verb *be*

2 (Circle) the correct form of the verb *be*.

Hi, my name ¹(*is*) / *are* Alicia. My favourite colour ²*is* / *are* blue. I ³*are* / *am* 12 years old. My best friends ⁴*is* / *are* Laura and Eva. They ⁵*isn't* / *aren't* from Mexico like me, they come from China. We ⁶*is* / *are* at school today.

3 Match questions 1–6 with answers a–f.

1 Are you hungry? [d]
2 Is your school big? [ ]
3 Is he in the room? [ ]
4 Is she from China? [ ]
5 Are we 12 years old? [ ]
6 Are they Canadian? [ ]

a Yes, we are.
b No, she isn't.
c No, it isn't.
d Yes, I am!
e No, they aren't.
f Yes, he is.

Question words

4 Complete the conversation with the words in the box.

How old   When   ~~Where~~   Who

A: Hi, Mateo. ¹ _Where_ are you from?
B: I'm from Argentina.
A: ² _____ are you?
B: I'm 13.
A: ³ _____ 's your birthday?
B: It's in February.
A: ⁴ _____ 's your favourite singer?
B: Taylor Swift. She's great!

whose + possessive pronouns

5 Write the words in the correct order to make questions. Then complete the answers with the correct possessive pronouns.

1 book / is / Whose / this /?
   Whose book is this?
   It's my book. It's ___mine.___

2 is / this / Whose / dictionary / ?
   _____
   It's your dictionary. It's _____

3 calculator / is / Whose / that / ?
   _____
   It's his calculator. It's _____

4 these / pens / Whose / are / ?
   _____
   They're her pens. They're _____

5 notebooks / those / are / Whose / ?
   _____
   They're our notebooks. They're _____

6 desks / are / Whose / those / ?
   _____
   They're their desks. They're _____

Imperatives

6 Write the affirmative or the negative.

1 Write on the paper.
   Don't write on the paper.

2 _____
   Don't use your calculator.

3 Use your dictionary, please.
   _____

4 _____
   Don't listen to your teacher.

5 Close the door, please.
   _____

6 _____
   Don't do your homework.

have got: affirmative and negative

Affirmative		Negative	
I've got		I haven't got	
You've got		You haven't got	
He's / She's / It's got	two brothers.	He / She / It hasn't got	three sisters.
We've got		We haven't got	
You've got		You haven't got	
They've got		They haven't got	

- We use **have got** to talk about possession.
  I've got five cousins.   She's got 12 grandchildren.

- We usually use contractions in conversation.
  He's got an aunt in Mexico City.
  They've got a photo of our grandfather.

- We use the full form of the verb **have got** to be more formal.
  He has got an aunt in Mexico City.
  They have got a photo of our grandfather.

- To make the negative, we put **n't** (not) after **have** and before **got**.
  We haven't got a big house.   She hasn't got a sister.

Possessive *'s*

Singular nouns	Plural nouns	Irregular plural nouns
Beth's computer	His parents' house	The women's football team
Carlos's bike	The students' books	The children's favourite toy

- We use **apostrophe + s** to indicate possession.
  This is Andrea's notebook.

- We put **'s** after a singular name or noun and **s'** after a plural name or noun.
  Carla's phone (NOT ~~The phone of Carla.~~)
  His grandparents' house (NOT ~~The house of his grandparents.~~)

- Some plural nouns are irregular. To show possession, we add **'s**.
  men's, people's, children's

- When two people possess something, we use **'s** after the second noun.
  Juan and Ana's family.
  Mum and Dad's computer.

have got: questions

Question		Short answer	
		Affirmative	Negative
Have	I got a blue book? you got a blue book?	Yes, I have. Yes, you have.	No, I haven't. No, you haven't.
Has	he / she / it got a blue book?	Yes, he / she / it has.	No, he / she / it hasn't.
Have	we got a blue book? you got a blue book? they got a blue book?	Yes, we have. Yes, you have. Yes, they have.	No, we haven't. No, you haven't. No, they haven't.

- We use **have** + **subject** + **got** + **object** in questions.
  Have you got a bike? Has your mum got a cousin?

- In spoken English, we reply to questions with short answers.
  A: *Have you got a brother?*
  B: *Yes, I have.* (NOT *Yes, I have* ~~got~~.) / *No, I haven't.* (NOT *No, I haven't* ~~got~~.)

How many ... have you got?

- We use **how many** + **object** + **have** + **subject** + **got** in questions to ask about the number of things.
  A: *How many cousins has he got?*   **B:** *He's got 30.*
  A: *How many brothers and sisters have you got?*   **B:** *I've got two sisters. I haven't got a brother.*

LANGUAGE PRACTICE

have got: affirmative and negative

1 Complete the sentences with the correct affirmative form of *have got*.

1 I _____have got_____ a dictionary.
2 We _____ six red pens.
3 My aunt _____ three sisters.
4 Mum and Dad _____ a mobile home.
5 You _____ 12 cousins.
6 Our house _____ five bedrooms.

2 Write the sentences in the negative.

1 I've got two brothers.
   I haven't got two brothers.
2 We've got a new teacher at school.
   _____
3 My grandma's got ten grandchildren.
   _____
4 My best friends have got green uniforms.
   _____
5 He's got a bike.
   _____
6 We've got a big house.
   _____

3 Look at the table and complete the text with the correct form of *have got*. Use contractions where possible.

	Juan	Rosa
sisters	1	2
brothers	0	1
cousins	2	2
bike	1	0
computer	0	0

Juan ¹ _'s got_ one sister, her name is Cecilia. He ² _____ any brothers. He ³ _____ a blue bike. Rosa ⁴ _____ two sisters and one brother. She ⁵ _____ a bike. Juan and Rosa ⁶ _____ two cousins. They ⁷ _____ a computer.

Possessive *'s*

4 Write *s'* or *'s* in the correct places in the sentences.

1 My dad bike is grey and my uncle bike is black.
   My dad's bike is grey and my uncle's bike is black.
2 Natalia favourite colour is green and her sister is blue.
   _____
3 His grandparent house is big but his parent house is small.
   _____
4 Myra family are from India and José family are from Spain.
   _____
5 Juan and Maria English book is red. Their mum book is yellow.
   _____

have got: questions

5 Write the words in the correct order to make questions. Then match them with answers (a–e).

1 got / I / Have / book / an / English / ?
   Have I got an English book?   d
2 bike / a / Have / blue / got / you / ?
   _____
3 pets / Alex / Has / two / got / ?
   _____
4 Catalina / brother / got / a / Has / ?
   _____
5 big / got / house / Have / they / a / ?
   _____

a Yes, he has. He's got two cats.   ~~d Yes, you have~~.
b No, she hasn't. She's got a sister.   e No, I haven't. It's green.
c Yes, they have.

How many ... have you got?

6 Write questions with *How many* for the answers.

1 How many cousins have you got?
   I've got three cousins.
2 _____
   My mum's got two nephews.
3 _____
   We've got 20 teachers at our school.
4 _____
   My best friend's got two sisters.
5 _____
   We've got four subjects on Friday at school.

Present simple: affirmative and negative

Affirmative	
I live	
You live	in Istanbul.
He / She / It lives	
We / You / They live	
Negative	
I don't live	
You don't live	in Istanbul.
He / She / It doesn't live	
We / You / They don't live	

- We use the present simple to talk about facts, habits and routines.
  I speak Chinese.   He goes to school. They study English.

- We form the negative of the present simple with the **subject** + **don't** / **doesn't** + **infinitive**.
  They don't speak English.

- We use **doesn't** in the third person (*he / she / it*).
  He doesn't do his homework.

Spelling: third person

- The third person form (*he / she / it*) of the present simple ends in **-s**.
  eat – he eats   read – she reads

- With verbs ending in **consonant** + **y**, we replace the **y** with **-ies** for the *he / she / it* forms.
  study – she studies

- The *he / she / it* form of verbs ending in **-ss**, **-sh**, **-ch**, **-x** and **-o** is **-es**.
  kiss – she kisses   relax – he relaxes finish – he finishes   go – she goes teach – she teaches

- Some verbs have got an irregular spelling in the third person.
  have – she has   be – he is

Adverbs of frequency

always   usually   often   sometimes   never
100% ←   → 0%

- Adverbs of frequency say how often we do something. They go after the verb *be* but before all other verbs.
  She's always happy.   He sometimes checks his phone in the afternoons. We usually do homework after school.

- With **never**, we always use an affirmative verb.
  I never go out with my friends on Monday.

- In questions, adverbs of frequency always come after the subject.
  Do you always have English class on Wednesday?

Present simple: questions

Question		Short answer	
		Affirmative	Negative
Do	I like oranges? you like oranges?	Yes, I do. Yes, you do.	No, I don't. No, you don't.
Does	he / she / it like oranges?	Yes, he / she / it does.	No, he / she / it doesn't.
Do	we like oranges? you like oranges? they like oranges?	Yes, we do. Yes, you do. Yes, they do.	No, we don't. No, you don't. No, they don't.

- We form present simple **Yes/No** questions with **do/does** + **subject** + **infinitive**.
  Do you brush your teeth in the morning? Does she go to bed at 9 pm?

- We use short answers with *do/does*. We don't repeat the main verb.
  A: *Do you often go to school by car?* **B:** *Yes, I do.*
  A: *Does he live in London?*   **B:** *No, he doesn't.*

Wh- questions

Question word	do/does	Subject	Verb
Who	do	you	live (with)?
What time	does	the party	start?
Where	does	she	live?
What	does	his dad	do?
When	do	they	play?

- We form **Wh-** questions with a **question word** + **do/does** + **subject** + **verb**.
  What time do you go to bed? (NOT *What time you go to bed?*)
  Where does he go to school?

- We also use the question **How often …?** to ask about frequency.
  How often do you play video games?

LANGUAGE PRACTICE

Present simple: affirmative and negative

1 Write the words in the correct order to make sentences.

1 I / every / day / wake / up / at / 7 pm
   I wake up at 7 pm every day.

2 gets / up / has / a / Antonio / shower / when / he
   _____

3 have / homework / Marina / Mondays / doesn't / on
   _____

4 don't / brothers / My / at / 8.30 pm / to / bed / go
   _____

5 lunch / school / We / have / at
   _____

6 my / with / homework / helps / My / dad / me
   _____

2 Complete the text with the present simple form of the verbs in brackets.

On Saturday mornings, Nehir [1] *gets up* (get up) at 9 am. She [2]_____ (have) a shower and [3]_____ (brush) her teeth. Then she [4]_____ (get dressed) and [5]_____ (have) her favourite breakfast: toast and fruit juice. She [6]_____ (not see) her dad on Saturday mornings because he [7]_____ (go) to work.

At 10 am she [8]_____ (go) to see her best friends, Beren and Ela. They [9]_____ (not live) near Nehir. She [10]_____ (go) on the bus to see them. Nehir [11]_____ (stay) at their house for about two hours, then she [12]_____ (get) the bus to her grandma's house. She [13]_____ (visit) her grandma on Saturdays because she [14]_____ (not see) her during the week.

Adverbs of frequency

3 (Circle) the correct options.

1 I... early in the morning.
   (a) usually get up   b get up usually

2 I... sports at the weekend.
   a do often   b often do

3 I... lunch with my sister at school.
   a sometimes have   b have sometimes

4 I... my homework in the evening.
   a do always   b always do

5 I... burgers for dinner.
   a never eat   b eat never

Present simple: questions

4 Complete the questions and answers. Use the verbs in brackets.

1 ___*Do*___ you ___*play*___ tennis at the weekend? (play)
   No, I ___*don't*___ .

2 _____ your cousin _____ to your school? (go)
   Yes, he _____! He's in my class.

3 _____ your parents _____ Spanish? (speak)
   No, they _____ .

4 _____ you often _____ your phone? (check)
   Yes, I _____ .

5 _____ your aunt _____ in England? (live)
   No, she _____ .

6 _____ your sister _____ her school uniform? (like)
   Yes, she _____ .

Wh- questions

5 Complete the questions with the words in the box.

| How often   What   What time   ~~When~~   Where   Who |

1 ___When___ do you go to school?

2 _____ do your aunt and uncle live?

3 _____ does your dad do?

4 _____ do you walk to school with?

5 _____ do you have exams at school?

6 _____ does your mum get up?

6 Match the answers (a–f) with the questions in Exercise 5.

a My best friend.   4

b From Monday to Friday.   ____

c In front of my house!   ____

d Every month!   ____

e He's an English teacher!   ____

f At seven o'clock during the week
   and eight o'clock at the weekend.   ____

can for ability and permission

Affirmative		Negative	
I		I	
You		You	
He / She / It	can play the piano.	He / She / It	can't play the piano.
We		We	
You		You	
They		They	

- We use **can** to express ability or permission.
  He can play the guitar. (ability)
  Dad says we can play video games tonight.
  (permission)
- **Can** is the same in all forms. The *he/she/it* form doesn't end in **-s**.
  She can speak Portuguese.
- We always use the infinitive without **to** after **can**.
  They can go to school.
  (NOT *They can to go to school.*)

can: questions

Yes/No questions	Short answer	
	Affirmative	Negative
Can I go?	Yes, I can.	No, I can't.
Can you go?	Yes, you can.	No, you can't.
Can he / she / it go?	Yes, he / she / it can.	No, he / she / it can't.
Can we go?	Yes, we can.	No, we can't.
Can you go?	Yes, you can.	No, you can't.
Can they go?	Yes, they can.	No, they can't.

- We change the word order when we form questions. We don't use **do/does**.
  Can you use your dictionary at school?
  (NOT *Do you can use your dictionary at school?*)
- We use the adverbs **very well**, **well**, **quite well**, **not very well**, **badly** or **not at all** to describe how we are able to do things.
  A: *Can you play the guitar?* **B:** *Yes, but not very well.*

Verb forms: (don't) like, don't mind, love, hate + -ing

- We use the **-ing** form of the verb after **like**, **don't like**, **don't mind**, **love** and **hate**.
  She loves reading books. (NOT *She loves read books.*)
  I don't mind going to school. (NOT *I don't mind go to school.*)
- We can also use nouns after these verbs.
  They don't mind geography but they love history.

Object pronouns

Subject pronoun	I	you	he	she	it	we	you	they
Object pronoun	me	you	him	her	it	us	you	them

- We use object pronouns after some verbs and prepositions.
  She meets <u>my sister and I</u> after school every day. – She meets <u>us</u> after school every day.
  I usually have lunch with <u>my friends</u>. – I usually have lunch with <u>them</u>.
- For animals and things, we use **it** (singular) and **them** (plural).
  Don't feed the bird! – Don't feed it!
  Do you read books? – Do you read them?
- We can also put an object pronoun after **like**, **don't like**, **don't mind**, **love** and **hate**.
  This is my new book. Do you like it? (NOT *Do you like?*)
  I don't like Mondays. I hate them.

LANGUAGE PRACTICE

can for ability and permission

1 Write sentences with *can*. Then write *A* (ability) or *P* (permission).

1 Artem / sing / very well
   Artem can sing very well.   A

2 My dad / speak / French
   _____   ____

3 I / use / my dad's / computer / in the evening
   _____   ____

4 My brother / dance / well
   _____   ____

5 Harry / play / the guitar well
   _____   ____

6 You / use my / phone
   _____   ____

2 Change the sentences in Exercise 1 to the negative.

1 Artem can't sing very well. _____
2 _____
3 _____
4 _____
5 _____
6 _____

can: questions

3 Look at the table and write questions and answers about Alberto and Sara.

	Alberto	Sara
take good photos	✔	✘
paint well	✘	✔
dance salsa	✔	✘

1 Can Alberto take good photos?   Yes, he can.
2 _____   _____
3 _____   _____
4 _____   _____
5 _____   _____
6 _____   _____

Verb forms: (don't) like, don't mind, love, hate + -ing

4 Complete the text with the words in brackets.
My sister ¹ *loves going* (love / go) to school.
She ² _____ (like / study). I'm different!
I ³ _____ (love / see) my friends at school.
I ⁴ _____ (not mind / learn) new things,
but I ⁵ _____ (not like / take) exams and
I ⁶ _____ (hate / get up) early every day!

Object pronouns

5 Match questions 1–5 with answers a–e. Then ⬭circle⬭ the correct object pronouns.

1 Do you like listening to your teacher?   b
2 Does your brother talk a lot?   ____
3 Do you love hanging out with your friends? ____
4 Can your friends help you and your sister? ____
5 Do you always go to judo classes?   ____

a Yes, he does, but I don't listen to *it / him*.
b Yes, I love listening to *me / her*.
c Yes, and my cousin comes to classes with *him / me*.
d Yes, I do. I meet *them / it* every day.
e No, they can't help *us / you*.

6 Rewrite the sentences with the object pronouns in the box.

| her | him | it | them | t̶h̶e̶m̶ | us |

1 I like hanging out with my friends.
  I like hanging out with them.
2 I can't find my pen.
  _____
3 I like my aunt.
  _____
4 They can't see you or me.
  _____
5 I love chatting online to my cousin, David!
  _____
6 I visit my grandparents on Sundays.
  _____

Countable and uncountable nouns

- Countable nouns can be counted individually. They have a singular and a plural form.
one apple – two apples   one book – three books
- Uncountable nouns can't be counted individually. They don't have a plural and are always singular.
bread (NOT ~~a bread~~)   *milk* (NOT ~~a milk~~)   *homework* (NOT ~~a homework~~)   *music* (NOT ~~a music~~)

a/an, some/any

	Singular countable	Plural countable	Uncountable
Affirmative	I've got an orange.	I've got some tomatoes.	I've got some chocolate.
Negative	I haven't got an orange.	I haven't got any tomatoes.	I haven't got any chocolate.
Question	Have you got an orange?	Have you got any tomatoes?	Have you got any chocolate?

- We use **a** with singular countable nouns.
a banana   a cat   a snack
- We use **an** with singular countable nouns when the noun starts with a vowel sound.
an orange   an uncle

- We use **some** and **any** when we don't know a quantity or it's not important.
- We use **some** and **any** with plural countable nouns. **Some** is usually used in affirmative sentences and **any** in negative sentences and questions.
We need some apples.   He hasn't got any tomatoes.   Have we got any carrots?
- We also use **some** and **any** with uncountable nouns. **Some** is usually used in affirmative sentences and **any** in negative sentences and questions.
We need some juice.   Marta hasn't got any water.   Have we got any rice?

there is/isn't, there are/aren't

	Singular	Plural
Affirmative	There's a quiz today.	There are some eggs on the table.
Negative	There isn't a quiz today.	There aren't any eggs on the table.
Question	Is there a quiz today?	Are there any eggs on the table?
Short answer	Yes, there is. No, there isn't.	Yes, there are. No, there aren't.

- We use **there is** with singular countable and uncountable nouns.
There is a school.
There is some cheese. (NOT *There ~~are~~ some cheese.*)
- We use **there are** with plural countable nouns.
There are some potatoes.   There are four pizzas.
- In questions and negatives we usually use **any** with plural countable and uncountable nouns.
Are there any bananas?   Is there any milk?
There aren't any burgers.   There isn't any bread.
- In informal English we can use the contraction **there's** but we don't use a contraction for **there are**.

much/many, a lot of

	Countable plural	Uncountable
Affirmative	There are a lot of eggs.	There's a lot of cheese.
Negative	There aren't many eggs.	There isn't much cheese.
Question	How many eggs are there?	How much cheese is there?

- We use **much**, **many** and **a lot of** to express quantity.
- We use **much** in negative sentences with uncountable nouns.
There isn't much water.
- We use **many** in negative sentences with countable nouns.
There aren't many tomatoes.
- We use **a lot of** in affirmative sentences with plural countable and uncountable nouns to describe a big quantity of something.
There are a lot of vegetables.   We've got a lot of rice.
- We use **how many** with plural countable nouns and **how much** with uncountable nouns to ask about quantity.
How many carrots are there?   How much juice have you got?

LANGUAGE PRACTICE

Countable and uncountable nouns

1 (Circle) the correct options.

1 I've got an (apple) / oranges in my school bag.
2 Alba's got some potato / meat for lunch.
3 I've got a banana / bread.
4 He hasn't got an cheese / egg for breakfast.
5 We haven't got any chocolate / carrot.
6 They've got some pear / milk.

a/an, some/any

2 Complete the sentences with a, an, some or any.

1 We need __some__ milk and __some__ eggs.
2 I've got _____ apple and _____ cheese for lunch.
3 Have you got _____ oranges, Mum? I want to make _____ orange juice.
4 We can't make a cake! We haven't got _____ eggs!
5 I want to make a sandwich. I need _____ tomato and _____ egg.
6 Let's buy _____ fizzy drink and _____ fruit at the supermarket.

there is/isn't, there are/aren't

3 Complete the conversation with the correct form of there is / there are.

A: Let's make a salad!
B: ¹ __Are there__ any tomatoes?
A: Yes ² _____, but ³ _____ any onions.
B: OK, that's not a problem. ⁴ _____ some cheese and ⁵ _____ ten carrots.
A: I don't want ten carrots in my salad! Let's make spaghetti!
B: Sorry! ⁶ _____ any pasta!

4 Write sentences about the food and drink in the box. Use the correct form of there is/there are and some or any.

> apples ✔ bread ✗ pizzas ✔ eggs ✗ water ✔ banana ✗

1 _There are some apples._
2 _____
3 _____
4 _____
5 _____
6 _____

much/many, a lot of

5 (Circle) the correct options. Then match questions 1–5 with answers a–f.

1 How (much) / many fruit do you eat every day? [e]
2 How much / many people are there in your family? [ ]
3 Do you spend much / many time checking your phone? [ ]
4 How many / much sweets do you have every day? [ ]
5 How much / many water do you drink at home? [ ]
6 Are there much / many bottles of fizzy drinks in your fridge? [ ]

a There are seven: I've got a lot of brothers and sisters!
b About two litres a day – more if I play tennis.
c There aren't any. We only drink water and milk at home.
d No! I haven't got much time to look at it!
e ~~I eat an apple every morning~~.
f I don't eat any! They're bad for my teeth!

LANGUAGE REFERENCE

Present continuous: affirmative and negative

Affirmative		Negative	
I'm		I'm not	
You're		You're not	
He's / She's / It's	eating dinner.	He's / She's / It's not	eating dinner.
We're		We're not	
You're		You're not	
They're		They're not	

- We use the present continuous to talk about actions in progress at the time of speaking.
  You are reading this sentence.
- For the affirmative, we use **subject** + **be** + **verb** + **-ing**.
  The dog is sleeping.   The children are playing.
- For the negative, we put **not** after **be**.
  She is not (isn't) downloading songs.

Present continuous: questions

(Question word)	*be*	Subject	Verb + *ing*
-	Am	I	reading?
-	Are	you	thinking?
-	Is	he / she / it	sleeping?
-	Are	we / you / they	learning?
What	are	you	doing?
Where	is	she	going?

Short answer	
Affirmative	**Negative**
Yes, I am.	No, I'm not.
Yes, you are.	No, you aren't.
Yes, he / she / it is.	No, he / she / it isn't.
Yes, we / you / they are.	No, we / you / they aren't.

- To form questions, we use **be** + **subject** + **verb** + **-ing**.
  Are you listening?
- We don't use the **verb** + **-ing** in short answers.
  Yes, I am. (NOT *Yes, I am listening.*)
- We form information questions with the **Wh-** question word before *be*.
  Who are you talking to?   What are they doing?

Spelling: *-ing* form

- With most verbs, we add **-ing** to the infinitive.
  eat – eating   read – reading   think – thinking
- For verbs ending in **-e**, we remove the **-e** and add **-ing**.
  write – writing   have – having   give – giving
- For verbs ending in a vowel and a consonant, we double the final consonant and add **-ing**.
  stop – stopping   shop – shopping
  plan – planning

Present simple and present continuous

- We use the present simple to talk about facts, habits and routines.
  Red and yellow make orange.
  I read a lot of books.
  He usually wears boots.
- We use the present continuous to talk about actions in progress at the time of speaking.
  I read a lot of books. At the moment, I'm reading a really good one.
  He usually wears boots, but he's wearing trainers today.
- Some verbs are not usually used in the continuous form: **hate**, **know**, **like**, **love**, **need**, **remember**, **think**, **understand**, **want**.
  I like that song. (NOT *I'm liking that song.*)
- We use expressions like **at the moment** and **right now** with the present continuous.
  He's playing video games at the moment.

LANGUAGE PRACTICE

Present continuous: affirmative and negative

1 Write the *-ing* form of the verbs.

1 eat ____eating____

2 write _____

3 chat _____

4 play _____

5 swim _____

6 have _____

2 Complete the sentences with the present continuous form of the verbs in the box.

> chat   get dressed   have   listen   ~~read~~   use

1 Luis ____is reading____ a book.

2 My grandparents _____ their dinner.

3 The teacher _____ to our stories.

4 My mum _____ to go to a party this evening.

5 You _____ my computer and I need it!

6 I _____ to my friends online.

3 Rewrite the sentences in Exercise 2 in the negative form of the present continuous. Use contractions.

1 Luis isn't reading a book._____

2 _____

3 _____

4 _____

5 _____

6 _____

Present continuous: questions

4 Complete the questions with the present continuous form of the verbs in brackets. Then write the short answers.

1 ____Are____ you ____doing____ (do) your homework?
Yes, ____I am.____

2 _____ your sister _____ (read) a book?
No, _____

3 _____ your uncle _____ (make) dinner?
Yes, _____

4 _____ we _____ (have) sandwiches for lunch?
No, _____

5 _____ my grandparents _____ (watch) TV?
No, _____

6 _____ the cat _____ (sleep) on my bed?
Yes, _____

Present simple and present continuous

5 Complete the rules. Write *present continuous* or *present simple*.

1 To talk about facts, routines and habits, we use the _____.

2 To talk about an action in progress at the time of speaking, we use the _____.

3 We use *always*, *often*, *usually*, *sometimes* and *never* with the _____.

4 We use *right now* and *at the moment* with the _____.

6 (Circle) the correct options.
My name is Carolina. At the moment, I'm on holiday and I [1]*help* / (*'m helping*) my dad. We have a big garden and he usually [2]*works* / *is working* all the time, so he's tired at the weekend. Now he is on holiday, too. I [3]*like* / *'m liking* flowers, and we usually [4]*collect* / *are collecting* some to put in the house. Right now my dad [5]*paints* / *is painting* the garden wall and, of course, my brother [6]*watches* / *is watching* us do all the work!

Comparatives

Comparatives	
Short adjectives smart	add -**er**: smarter
Short adjectives ending in vowel + consonant big	double the final consonant and add -**er**: bigger
Adjectives ending in -e safe	add -r: safer
Adjectives ending in -y easy	remove the -**y** and add -**ier**: easier
Long adjectives interesting	put **more** before the adjective: more interesting
Irregular adjectives good bad	better worse

- We use comparative adjectives to compare one thing with another. We use the verb **be** + **a comparative adjective** + **than**.
  José is taller than his father.

Superlatives

Superlatives	
Short adjectives smart	add -**est** smartest
Short adjectives ending in vowel + consonant big	double the final consonant and add -**est**: biggest
Adjectives ending in -e safe	add -**est**: safest
Adjectives ending in -y easy	remove the -**y** and add -**iest**: easiest
Long adjectives interesting	put **most** before the adjective: most interesting
Irregular adjectives good bad	best worst

- We use superlative adjectives to say a thing or person has got the most of a particular quality. We use **the** with a **superlative adjective**.
  José is the tallest person in his family.

LANGUAGE PRACTICE

Comparatives

1 Match the adjectives with their opposites.

1 big   [d]   a unhealthy
2 boring   [ ]   b short
3 easy   [ ]   c new
4 tall   [ ]   d ~~small~~
5 old   [ ]   e difficult
6 healthy   [ ]   f interesting

2 Write the comparative form of the adjectives in the box next to the comparative with the same spelling rule.

> bad   comfortable   heavy   nice   ~~old~~   thin

1 smarter   _older_
2 bigger   _____
3 safer   _____
4 easier   _____
5 more interesting   _____
6 better   _____

3 Write sentences with comparatives about Zehra's family.

1 My sister / short / me
My sister is shorter than me.

2 My brother / young / me
_____

3 My sister / funny / my brother
_____

4 My mum / thin / my dad
_____

5 My brother / old / my sister
_____

6 My / cousin / intelligent / me
_____

Superlatives

4 Complete the table with the superlative.

Adjective	Comparative	Superlative
high	higher	1 _the highest_
amazing	more amazing	2 _____
easy	easier	3 _____
bad	worse	4 _____
popular	more popular	5 _____
big	bigger	6 _____

5 Complete the sentences with the superlative form of the adjectives in brackets.

1 I think my dad is the _____best_____ (good) dad in the world.
2 Many footballers are the _____ (rich) people in sport.
3 My mum says Formula 1 racing is the _____ (fast) sport.
4 This is the _____ (heavy) bag in the world! What have you got in it?
5 I think ice hockey is one of the _____ (dangerous) sports.
6 Which is the _____ (easy) sport to learn?

6 Complete the text with the comparative or superlative form of the adjectives in brackets.

On Saturdays I usually go and see my cousin play football. She's [1] _____the best_____ (good) player in the team. She always scores [2] _____ (amazing) goals! She's [3] _____ (tall) player in the team and she's [4] _____ (fast) than the others. I think she's also [5] _____ (intelligent) than her team mates because she watches what is happening all the time! She's also [6] _____ (popular) player in the team!

was/were

Affirmative		Negative	
I / He / She / It	was good.	I / He / She / It	wasn't good.
You / We / They	were good.	You / We / They	weren't good.
Question		Short answer	
		Affirmative	Negative
Was I / he / she / it good?		Yes, I / he / she / it was.	No, I / he / she / it wasn't.
Were you / we / they good?		Yes, you / we / they were.	No, you / we / they weren't.

- **Was** and **were** are the past simple forms of **be**.
  There was a special gorilla in Barcelona zoo.
  The elephants were born without tusks.

- To form questions, we use **was/were**. We don't use **do**.
  Was he a white tiger? (NOT ~~Does he was a white tiger?~~)
  Were the elephants enormous?

- We form information questions with the **Wh-** question before **was/were**.
  What was it?   Where were you last night?

there was/were

	Affirmative	Negative
Singular	There was a gorilla at the zoo.	There wasn't a gorilla at the zoo.
Plural	There were three lions.	There weren't three lions.
Question	Short answer	
	Affirmative	Negative
Was there a gorilla at the zoo?	Yes, there was.	No, there wasn't.
Were there three lions?	Yes, there were.	No, there weren't.

- **There was**/**were** are the past simple forms of **there is**/**are**.
  There was a park here.   There were two cars.

- We use **there was** with singular countable nouns and uncountable nouns.
  There was a pen here.   There was some milk in the fridge.

- We use **there were** with plural countable nouns.
  There were a lot of tourists in our town last weekend.

- In questions and negatives, we usually use **any** with plural countable and uncountable nouns
  Were there any interesting animals at the zoo?
  Was there any bread at home?
  There weren't any cats.   There wasn't any rice.

Past simple: regular and irregular verbs

- We use the past simple to talk about completed events and actions in the past.
  I played basketball yesterday.
  He lived in London last year.

Spelling

most verbs	add -**ed**: *show – showed*
verbs ending in -**e**	add -**d**: *live – lived*
verbs ending in **consonant + -y**	remove the -**y** and add -**ied**: *study – studied*
verbs ending in **consonant + vowel + consonant**	double the final consonant and add -**ed**: *shop – shopped* *stop – stopped*

Irregular verbs

- Irregular past simple verbs don't follow any pattern.
  get – got   do – did   see – saw   have – had

Past simple: negative

	didn't	Infinitive	Other words
I / You / He / She / It / You / We / They	didn't	play	football yesterday.
		go	to the cinema.

- To form the past simple negative, we use **subject + didn't + infinitive** without **to**.
  Javier didn't watch TV last night.
  They didn't have lunch at home today.

- We can use time expressions such as **yesterday**, **last night**, **last weekend** and **last summer** with the past simple. We usually put them at the end of a sentence.
  We went to a safari park last weekend.

- We use **ago** with the past simple to talk about when something happened. We usually put it at the end of a sentence.
  Alex arrived home two hours ago.

was/were

1 (Circle) the correct options.

1 The monkey (was) / were in a tree at the zoo.

2 The baby elephant *was / were* beautiful!

3 The bears *wasn't / weren't* very big, but the lions *was / were* enormous!

4 It *wasn't / weren't* a very interesting documentary – it *was / were* very boring!

5 We *was / were* at the zoo for hours!

6 Diego *was / were* happy but Maria *wasn't / weren't*!

2 Put the words in the correct order to make questions. Then complete the answers with *was* or *were*.

1 happy / Maria / was / ?

A: Was Maria happy?

B: Yes, she ___was___ .

2 yesterday / were / Where / you / ?

A: _____

B: I _____ at home.

3 were / Who / with / you / ?

A: _____

B: My friend _____ at home with me.

4 the / zoo / Was / big / ?

A: _____

B: Yes, it _____ enormous!

5 most / What / animal / was / the / interesting / ?

A: _____

B: The tigers! They _____ beautiful.

there was/were

3 (Circle) the correct options.

For many years ¹*there wasn't /* (*there weren't*) many people in my town and ²*there wasn't / there weren't* a place to see animals, but in 2015 everything changed – ³*there was / there were* houses, people, children, shops and ⁴*there was / there were* a new animal park! ⁵*There wasn't / There weren't* any big animals, like elephants, but ⁶*there was / there were* lovely little animals, like rabbits and lots of different birds. Now, it's my favourite place!

Past simple: regular and irregular verbs

4 Write the past simple form of the verbs in the table

Regular	watch	live	hate
	¹ watched	² _____	³ _____
	plan	stop	study
	⁴ _____	⁵ _____	⁶ _____
Irregular	do	eat	get
	⁷ _____	⁸ _____	⁹ _____
	go	have	see
	¹⁰ _____	¹¹ _____	¹² _____

5 Complete the text with the past simple form of the verbs in brackets.

We ¹ _arrived_ (arrive) at the animal park in the morning. My little sister ² _____ (want) to see the birds, but they were at the other end of the park. She ³ _____ (cry) for a few minutes, then I ⁴ _____ (show) her the rabbits. She ⁵ _____ (love) them! She ⁶ _____ (play) with them for hours!

6 Write the words in the correct order to make sentences.

1 week / my / went / to / dad / mountains / Last / I / the / with

Last week I went to the mountains with my dad.

2 brown / bears / saw / big / We / two

_____

3 so / we / had / My / dad / a sandwich / was / hungry

_____

4 behind / I / bear / me / heard / a

_____

5 up / a / tree / I / went / bear / ate / my / sandwich / and / the

_____

6 My / the / ran / to / car / eat / his / sandwich, but / dad / didn't

_____

Past simple: questions

did	Subject	Infinitive	Short answer	
			Affirmative	**Negative**
Did	I / you / he / she / it / we / you / they	play?	Yes, I / you / he / she / it / we / you / they did.	No, I / you / he / she / it / we / you / they didn't.

- We make past simple questions with **did** + **subject** + **the infinitive**.
  Did she enjoy the yoga class?

Past simple: *Wh-* questions

Question word	did	Subject	Infinitive
Who			go with?
What time			go?
Where	did	I / you / he / she / it / we / you / they	go?
What			go for?
When			go?
How			go?

- We form *Wh-* questions in the past simple with a **question word** + **did** + **subject** + **the infinitive**.
  What time did you go to bed?
  Where did they go on holiday?
  What did you do at the weekend?
  Who did she see there?
  How did he feel?
  When did you arrive?

LANGUAGE PRACTICE

Past simple: questions

1 Match questions 1–5 with answers a–e.

1 Did you go to the post office this morning? [d]
2 Did you and Antonia watch TV last night? [ ]
3 Did the shop close early yesterday? [ ]
4 Did your friends go to the bowling alley with you? [ ]
5 Did our English teacher correct our homework? [ ]

a No, she didn't.   d Yes, I did.
b Yes, we did.   e No, it didn't.
c Yes, they did.

2 Look at the information about the activities Sergio and Andrea did at the weekend. Write short answers.

	Go bowling	Tidy bedroom	Visit grandparents	Go swimming
Sergio	✓	✗	✓	✗
Andrea	✗	✓	✓	✗

1 Did Sergio go bowling?   Yes, he did.
2 Did Sergio tidy his bedroom?   _____
3 Did Andrea tidy her bedroom?   _____
4 Did Sergio visit his grandparents?   _____
5 Did Andrea go swimming?   _____
6 Did Sergio go swimming?   _____

3 Write questions and short answers.

1 your cousins / see / the fish / at the / aquarium ✓
   A: Did your cousins see the fish at the aquarium?
   B: Yes, they did.

2 Daniel / go to / the skate park / yesterday ✗
   A: _____
   B: _____

3 you and Melody / meet / at the cinema / today ✓
   A: _____
   B: _____

4 Olga / do / judo / last year ✗
   A: _____
   B: _____

5 you / stay / at the hospital / for a long time ✓
   A: _____
   B: _____

Past simple: *Wh-* questions

4 Circle the correct options.

1 A: *What* / *Where* did you do at the weekend?
   B: I stayed at home.
2 A: *Where* / *When* did they play handball on Sunday?
   B: In the sports centre.
3 A: *What* / *Who* did he see at the ice rink?
   B: Nobody he knew.
4 A: *How* / *When* did he feel?
   B: Not very well.
5 A: *How* / *What* time did they leave?
   B: About 5 pm.
6 A: *When* / *Who* did they catch the train?
   B: Early this morning.

5 Complete the dialogue with *Wh-* question words from Exercise 4.

Yusaf: I like your phone. ¹ Where did you get it?

Ali: In the new shopping centre.

Yusaf: Was it expensive?

Ali: I don't know! It was a present.

Yusaf: ² _____ bought it for you?

Ali: My mum. She got it for my birthday!

Yusaf: Wow, that's a fantastic present! ³ _____ did she get it?

Ali: She got it last week when we went shopping, but I didn't see her buy it!

Yusaf: ⁴ _____ did you feel when you got it?

Ali: Surprised and happy!

Yusaf: ⁵ _____ did I get you? I can't remember!

Ali: Nothing, you forgot!

Yusaf: Sorry!

Future with *will/won't*

Affirmative		Negative		Question		Short answer	
						Affirmative	**Negative**
I/You/He/She/It/We /You/They	will pass the exam.	I/You/He/She/It/We /You/They	won't pass the exam.	Will I/you/he/she/it/we/you/they	pass the exam?	Yes, I/you/he/she/it/we/you/they will.	No, I/you/he/she/it/we/you/they won't.

- We use **will** and **won't** to make predictions about the future.
  Computers will control our lives in the future.

- **Will/Won't** doesn't change in the third person.

- We change the word order when we form questions. We don't use **do/does**.
  Will we travel in cars in the future?

- In informal English we use the contraction **'ll**.
  They'll sleep in a camper van on holiday.

Present continuous for future

- We can use the present continuous to talk about fixed arrangements in the future.
  I'm meeting my friend Maite at 6.30.
  My sister's travelling to Brazil in October.

- We often use future time expressions such as **tonight**, **tomorrow**, **this weekend**, **this summer**, **next week**, **next month** and **after class/school**.
  What are you doing tonight?
  We're travelling to Paris this summer.
  Is he coming to the party on Saturday?

be going to

Affirmative		Negative	
I'm		I'm not	
You're		You aren't	
He's		He isn't	
She's	going to run.	She isn't	going to run.
It's		It isn't	
We're		We aren't	
You're		You aren't	
They're		They aren't	

- We use **be going to** to talk about future plans and intentions.
  She's going to take her camera on holiday.
  I'm going to wear my new trainers.

- To form the affirmative, we use **be** + **going to** + **infinitive**.
  We're going to have dinner in a restaurant.

- To form the negative, we use **be** + **not** + **going to** + **infinitive**. **Not** is usually contracted.
  They aren't going to go on holiday this summer.

Question	Short answer	
	Affirmative	**Negative**
Am I going to be there?	Yes, I am.	No, I'm not.
Are you going to be there?	Yes, you are.	No, you aren't.
Is he going to be there?	Yes, he is.	No, he isn't.
Is she going to be there?	Yes, she is.	No, she isn't.
Is it going to be there?	Yes, it is.	No, it isn't.
Are we going to be there?	Yes, we are.	No, we aren't.
Are you going to be there?	Yes, you are.	No, you aren't.
Are they going to be there?	Yes, they are.	No, they aren't.

- We form questions with **be** before the subject.
  Is he going to tell us the answers to the homework?

- We form information questions with a **Wh-** question word before **be**.
  Who is he going to ask?
  What are you going to wear to the party?
  Why is Susana going to be late?

LANGUAGE PRACTICE

Future with *will/won't*

1 Complete the sentences about a camping trip. Write *'ll* or *won't*.

1 Don't sit at the bottom of the boat. You 'll_____ get wet.

2 Don't make the shelter. You _____ know how to do it.

3 Don't swim in the river. It's dangerous so you _____ be safe!

4 Don't eat and then swim. You _____ be sick!

5 Don't walk alone at night because you _____ get lost!

6 Don't lose your compass. You _____ know how to get back to the camp.

2 Write sentences with *will* or *won't* about the things you can do on holiday.

1 have a good time ✓   I will have a good time._____

2 get bored ✗   _____

3 go to the beach every day ✓   _____

4 stay in a tent ✗   _____

5 eat good food ✓   _____

6 do any homework ✗   _____

Present continuous for future

3 Complete the email with the present continuous form of the verbs in brackets.

Hi Sandra,

How are you? It's the school holidays next week! I ¹'m going (go) on an adventure trip and my sister ² _____ (come) too! In August my dad ³ _____ (take) me on a boat trip! My mum ⁴ _____ (not go) because she doesn't like boats! She ⁵ _____ (visit) my grandparents. I think you ⁶ _____ (fly) to England for a week. Is that right? What are you doing after that?

Jorge

4 Complete the sentences with the present continuous form of the verbs in the box.

| come   go   have   ~~meet~~   not visit   play |

1 I'm ___meeting___ my friends tomorrow morning.

2 When _____ you _____ basketball?

3 _____ grandad _____ for lunch on Sunday?

4 _____ Ben and Sam _____ a party next week?

5 We _____ my aunt and uncle this weekend.

6 Where _____ you _____ shopping on Friday?

be going to

5 Rewrite the sentences in the negative.

1 I'm going to see my grandma next week.

I'm not going to see my grandma next week._____

2 You are going to make new friends.

_____

3 Marina is going to visit the wildlife park next month.

_____

4 Mohammed is going to go to a summer camp next year.

_____

5 We are going to learn how to make a shelter.

_____

6 They are going to climb the mountain.

_____

6 Complete the conversations with the correct form of *be going to*. Use the verbs in brackets.

1 A: *What are you going to do* (do) in the school holidays?

B: I _____ (visit) my aunt in London.

2 A: _____ (he / stay) in a hotel?

B: No, he _____

3 A: _____ (Gabriel and Ana / climb) in the mountains?

B: Yes, they _____

4 A: We _____ (not go) on holiday this year.

B: _____ (you / stay) at home?

LANGUAGE BANK

STARTER

Vocabulary
Months

> January   February   March   April   May
> June   July   August   September
> October   November   December

Colours

> black   blue   green   orange   pink
> red   yellow   white

Classroom objects

> board   calculator   chair   dictionary
> door   notebook   pen   pencil   poster
> ruler   table   window

Language in action
Subject pronouns
Possessive adjectives
Verb *be*
Question words
whose + possessive pronouns
Imperatives

Writing
Useful language
An informal letter
To start: Dear + Mr (*man*) or Mrs/Miss (*woman*)
+ person's surname
To end: All the best, Best wishes
To join two ideas in one sentence: and

UNIT 1

Vocabulary
Family members

> aunt   brother   cousin   dad   daughter
> grandad   granddaughter   grandma
> grandson   husband   mum   nephew
> niece   sister   son   uncle   wife

Describing people
Eyes: brown, grey
Hairstyle: long, short, wavy
Hair colour: blonde, brown, grey, red
Height: tall, short
Other features: beard, glasses, freckles, moustache

Language in action
have got: affirmative, negative, questions and short
answers
how many … ?
Possessive *'s*

Speaking
Everyday English
Are you alright?
Cool!
Got to go!
That's funny!
That's so not funny!

Useful language
Bye!
Hey, (Evan)
Hi, (Lily)
How are things?
OK/Fine, thanks. You?
See you later.

Writing
Useful language
An informal email
at the start: Hi, Hey, Hello
at the end: Email me soon, That's all for now, Write
soon!
contractions: I'm, I've, He's, She's, We're, Here's,
Who's

LANGUAGE BANK

UNIT 2

Vocabulary
Daily routines

> brush your teeth   check your phone
> do your homework   get dressed
> go home   go to bed   go to school
> get up   have a shower   have breakfast
> pack your bag   wake up

Leisure activities

> chat online   download songs   go for a bike ride
> go shopping   hang out with friends
> listen to music   make videos
> play an instrument   play video games
> read a book/magazine   take photos   watch TV

Language in action
Present simple: affirmative and negative
Adverbs of frequency

Speaking
Everyday English
Go ahead.
It depends.
No problem.
Sure.
That's easy!

Useful language
Is that OK?
I've got one more question.
I've got some questions to ask you.
Thank you very much for your time.
That's interesting.

Writing
Useful language
An article
apostrophe **'**
comma **,**
capital letter **A, B, C**
exclamation mark **!**
full stop **.**
question mark **?**

UNIT 3

Vocabulary
School subjects

> art   design and technology (DT)   drama
> English   food technology   geography   history
> information and communication technology (ICT)
> maths   music   physical education (PE)
> science   Spanish

Places in a school

> canteen   classroom   ICT room   library
> locker area   main hall   playing field
> reception   science lab   sports hall
> staffroom   toilets

Language in action
can for ability and permission
Verb forms: (*don't*) *like*, *don't mind*, *love*, *hate* + *-ing*

Speaking
Everyday English
Don't be silly!
I'm stuck.
Not again!
Not great.
Oh, dear!

Useful language
Are you sure?
Can you do me a favour?
Can you help me, please?
Do you need a hand with …?

Writing
Useful language
A description
for example
like
such as

LANGUAGE BANK

UNIT 4

Vocabulary
Food and drink

| apples bananas beans carrots cheese
chicken chocolate eggs fish
fizzy drink juice meat rice water |

Adjectives to describe food

| cold delicious disgusting fresh healthy
hot nice salty sweet unhealthy |

Language in action
Countable and uncountable nouns
a/an, some/any
there isn't/aren't
much, many, a lot of

Speaking
Everyday English
Enjoy!
Here you go.
No problem.
No worries!

Useful language
Can I have …?
Can I help you?
How much is that?
I'd like a/an/some …
Is that everything?
That's …, please.
What kind?
What's in the …?

Writing
Useful language
A description
We use *and* to add similar information.
We use *but* to contrast different information.
We use *or* when there is a choice (usually between two things).

UNIT 5

Vocabulary
Clothes

| boots cap flip-flops hoodie jacket
jeans joggers shirt shorts
skirt T-shirt trainers |

Accessories

| belt bracelet earrings gloves necklace
purse ring scarf sunglasses umbrella
wallet watch |

Language in action
Present continuous
Present simple and present continuous

Speaking
Everyday English
It's a bargain.
It's perfect.
No, honestly.
You're in luck!

Useful language
Can I help you?
Can I see the … one, please?
Have you got it in a different (size/colour/style)?
I'm looking for …
It comes in …
What about this one / these?

Writing
Useful language
A description of a photo
at the back
in the middle
on the left/right
next to (someone)

LANGUAGE BANK

UNIT 6

Vocabulary
Sports

> athletics   basketball   (mountain/rock) climbing
> gymnastics   hockey   rugby   running
> sailing   swimming   table tennis
> volleyball   windsurfing   yoga

Sports verbs

> bounce   catch   climb   dive   hit   jump
> kick   lift   pass   run   score   throw

Language in action
Comparatives
Superlatives

Speaking
Everyday English
Got them!
Look!
That's crazy!
What are we waiting for?
Why not?

Useful language
How much are tickets?
Let's book them.
Let's go.
Shall we go?
They're (£45).
What's the (quickest/best/cheapest) way to get there?

Writing
Useful language
A profile of a sportsperson
We use *also* and *too* to give extra information.
We use *also* after the verb *be*.
We use *also* before other verbs.
We use *too* at the end of a sentence.

UNIT 7

Vocabulary
Animals

> **Birds:**
> duck   eagle   parrot
> **Mammals:**
> bear   donkey   giraffe   hippo   horse
> lion   monkey   mouse   whale
> **Reptiles:**
> crocodile   snake

Adjectives

> beautiful   clever   cute   dangerous   heavy
> huge   large   lazy   light   long
> noisy   quiet   safe   short   tiny   wild

Language in action
was/were, there was/were
Past simple: regular and irregular verbs

Speaking
Everyday English
No way!
Really?
Wow!
You're joking!

Useful language
How was (the school trip)?
It was (really amazing).
What about (lions)?
What was (it) like?

Writing
Useful language
A biography
A few years ago
In 2007
On 10 October 2005

LANGUAGE BANK

UNIT 8

Vocabulary
Places in town

> aquarium bowling alley car park
> cinema hospital ice rink post office
> shopping centre skate park sports centre
> swimming pool

Personal possessions

> bus pass camera concert ticket headphones
> IC card keys laptop money passport
> phone portable charger tablet

Grammar
Past simple: questions
Past simple: *Wh-* questions

Speaking
Everyday English
Calm down.
Don't panic!
Gross!
Let's drink.

Useful language
Did you have it when you (got to school)?
Did you put it (in your bag)?
What did you do with it after that?
When did you last (have/use/see) it?

Writing
Useful language
A blog post
I didn't hear my alarm **so** I got up late.

UNIT 9

Vocabulary
Outdoor life

> use a compass light a fire read a map
> build a shelter catch a fish
> find food and water pick fruit
> cook over a campfire identify plants
> collect wood

Holidays

> apartment bed & breakfast (B&B)
> camper van caravan chalet cottage
> hotel tent youth hostel

Grammar
Future with *will/won't*
Present continuous for future
be going to

Speaking
Everyday English
Easy!
Forget that.
I'm on it!
You're unbelievable!

Useful language
What about a (film night)?
What are we going to do?
Why don't we (have a picnic)?
I'm not sure about that.
I'd rather not do that.
Let's do that!

Writing
Useful language
An email
at home
in the morning
in August
on Monday
on 1 August
at the airport

IRREGULAR VERBS

Infinitive	Past simple
be	was / were
beat	beat
become	became
begin	began
break	broke
bring	brought
build	built
buy	bought
catch	caught
choose	chose
come	came
cost	cost
cut	cut
do	did
draw	drew
drink	drank
drive	drove
eat	ate
fall	fell
feel	felt
fight	fought
find	found
fly	flew
forget	forgot
get	got
give	gave
go	went
grow	grew
have	had
hear	heard
hide	hid
hit	hit
hold	held
keep	kept

Infinitive	Past simple
know	knew
leave	left
lose	lost
make	made
meet	met
pay	paid
put	put
read	read
ride	rode
ring	rang
run	ran
say	said
see	saw
sell	sold
send	sent
show	showed
shut	shut
sing	sang
sit	sat
sleep	slept
speak	spoke
spend	spent
stand	stood
swim	swam
take	took
teach	taught
tell	told
think	thought
throw	threw
understand	understood
wake	woke
wear	wore
win	won
write	wrote

Acknowledgements

The authors and publishers acknowledge the following sources of copyright material and are grateful for the permissions granted. While every effort has been made, it has not always been possible to identify the sources of all the material used, or to trace all copyright holders. If any omissions are brought to our notice, we will be happy to include the appropriate acknowledgements on reprinting and in the next update to the digital edition, as applicable.

Key: SU = Starter Unit, U = Unit.

Photography
All photographs are sourced from Getty Images.

SU: Radius Images; kali9/iStock/Getty Images Plus; Carol Yepes/Moment; Classen Rafael/EyeEm; s-cphoto/E+; RinoCdZ/iStock/Getty Images Plus; Classen Rafael/EyeEm; C Squared Studios/Photodisc; AigarsR/iStock/Getty Images Plus; **U1**: Westend61; abell7302/iStock/Getty Images Plus; m-imagephotography; Tempura/iStock/Getty Images Plus; Rafael Elias/Moment; SSC/Stone; Xose Casal Photography/Moment; Jose Luis Pelaez Inc/Blend Images; Gustavo Di Mario/The Image Bank; Anders Johansson/EyeEm; Floresco Productions/Cultura; Andrew Bret Wallis/The Image Bank; jane/iStock/Getty Images Plus; Kalle Singer; Juanmonino/iStock/Getty Images Plus; ImagesBazaar; Simon D. Warren/Corbis/VCG; Thomas Barwick/Taxi; Bruce Laurance/The Image Bank; Images Bazaar; aimintang/iStock/Getty Images Plus; **U2**: bamby-bhamby/iStock/Getty Images Plus; Klaus Vedfelt/DigitalVision; JGI/Jamie Grill/Blend Images; instamatic/iStock/Getty Images Plus; SolStock/iStock/Getty Images Plus; SolStock/E+; Jim Jordan Photography/The Image Bank; James Collins/Corbis; "Steve Debenport/E+; "Glenda Christina/Perspectives; FatCamera/E+; Lobro78/iStock/Getty Images Plus; Westend61; LeoPatrizi/E+; Robert Daly/Caiaimage; Morsa Images/DigitalVision; Jamie Grill/The Image Bank; JGI/Tom Grill/Blend Images; Juanmonino/iStock/Getty Images Plus; Nick David/Taxi/Getty Images Plus; **U3**: Jupiterimages/Stockbyte; YinYang/E+; Wavebreakmedia/iStock/Getty Images Plus; NikolayN/iStock/Getty Images Plus; uptonpark/iStock/Getty Images Plus; Klaus Vedfelt/Taxi; Jon Feingersh/Blend Images; Mint Images RF; Eri Morita/The Image Bank; Vanda9/iStock/Getty Images Plus; Compassionate Eye Foundation/London, United Kingdom; hartcreations/E+; Image Source; Dinodia Photo/Passage; Amos Morgan/Photodisc; alongoldsmith/RooM; **U4**: Dougal Waters/DigitalVision; letty17/iStock/Getty Images Plus; Theerawan Bangpran/iStock/Getty Images Plus; Derkien/iStock/Getty Images Plus; Magone/iStock/Getty Images Plus; rimglow/iStock/Getty Images Plus; Foodcollection RF; tc397/iStock/Getty Images Plus; MielPhotos2008/iStock/Getty Images Plus; vanillaechoes/iStock/Getty Images Plus; chengyuzheng/iStock/Getty Images Plus; ddukang/iStock/Getty Images Plus; Onegin/iStock/Getty Images Plus; Bartosz Luczak/iStock/Getty Images Plus; Astrakan Images/Cultura; imtmphoto/iStock/Getty Images Plus; Vladimir Godnik; Donald Iain Smith/Blend Images; Buena Vista Images/DigitalVision; Veronika Lipar/EyeEm; Axel Bueckert/EyeEm; Karly Pope/Moment Open; Arx0nt/iStock/Getty Images Plus; rez-art/iStock/Getty Images Plus; Teen00000/iStock/Getty Images Plus; Science Photo Library; IvanMikhaylov/iStock/Getty Images Plus; Simone_Capozzi/iStock/Getty Images Plus; joakimbkk/iStock/Getty Images Plus; Inmagineasia; Taiyou Nomachi/DigitalVision; **U5**: OxfordSquare/iStock/Getty Images Plus; s-cphoto/iStock/Getty Images Plus; primeimages/E+; mfto/iStock/Getty Images Plus; mawielobob/iStock/Getty Images Plus; akova/iStock/Getty Images Plus; traveler1116/iStock/Getty Images Plus; Bounce/Cultura; 3alexd/E+; macroworld/iStock/Getty Images Plus; Jordan Siemens/Iconica; Maskot; gradyreese/E+; FatCamera/iStock/Getty Images Plus; Richard Drury/DigitalVision;

Jeremy Woodhouse/Blend Images; **U6**: omgimages/iStock/Getty Images Plus; Frank-Ramspott/iStock/Getty Images Plus; Sam Kadiri/EyeEm; Hermann Erber/LOOK-foto; Meinzahn/iStock/Getty Images Plus; bowdenimages/iStock/Getty Images Plus; Cultura Exclusive/Rebecca Nelson; David Rogers/Getty Images Sport; Patrik Giardino/Corbis; gbh007/iStock/Getty Images Plus; Erik Isakson/Blend Images; Will Gray/AWL Images; Dennis Grombkowski/Getty Images Sport; Ramin Burhani/EyeEm; Echo/Juice Images; Foto Olimpik/NurPhoto; Feng Li/Getty Images Sport; Tim Clayton - Corbis/Corbis Sport; skynesher/E+; Markus Gann/EyeEm; Hero Images; Ty Allison/Photographer's Choice; lzf/iStock/Getty Images Plus; **U7**: Dugwy/iStock/Getty Images Plus; GlobalP/iStock/Getty Images Plus; mtruchon/iStock/Getty Images Plus; Alexey_Seafarer/iStock/Getty Images Plus; reisegraf/iStock/Getty Images Plus; PAUL J. RICHARDS/AFP; Chasing Light - Photography by James Stone james-stone.com/Moment; ROGER HARRIS/Science Photo Library; CoreyFord/iStock/Getty Images Plus; kavram/iStock/Getty Images Plus; SharafMaksumov/iStock/Getty Images Plus; Jim Cumming/Moment; Sudowoodo/iStock/Getty Images Plus; MariaArefyeva/iStock/Getty Images Plus; Quim Roser/Cultura; COffe72/iStock/Getty Images Plus; Justin Sullivan/Getty Images Entertainment; Handout/Australia Zoo/Getty Images Entertainment; Sean Fleming/EyeEm; Creative-Nature_nl/iStock/Getty Images Plus; Mostafa Gabr/EyeEm; ERNESTO BENAVIDES/AFP; Dennis George Booth/EyeEm; Paul A. Souders/Corbis Documentary; Jeffrey Coolidge/DigitalVision; Janos/iStock/Getty Images Plus; Tim Platt/Stone; Danita Delimont/Gallo Images; baronvsp/iStock/Getty Images Plus; Mr_Khan/iStock/Getty Images Plus; jashlock/iStock/Getty Images Plus; Barrie Thomas/EyeEm; Dave Fleetham/Design Pics/Perspectives; Anup Shah/Stockbyte; **U8**: fotovampir/iStock/Getty Images Plus; lkpg-foto/iStock/Getty Images Plus; GOLFX/iStock/Getty Images Plus; Alter_photo/iStock/Getty Images Plus; MandM_Photo/iStock/Getty Images Plus; Chalabala/iStock/Getty Images Plus; Weekend Images Inc/E+; PhotoAlto/Odilon Dimier/PhotoAlto Agency RF Collections; Fancy/Veer/Corbis; bbostjan/E+; Tobias Ackeborn/Moment Open; farakos/iStock/Getty Images Plus; urbancow/E+; PBNJ Productions/Blend Images; Steve Woods Photography/Cultura; duncan1890/DigitalVision Vectors; gresei/iStock/Getty Images Plus; luismmolina/iStock/Getty Images Plus; Creative Crop/DigitalVision; rustemgurler/iStock/Getty Images Plus; Jamie Grill; Michael Burrell/iStock/Getty Images Plus; cudger/iStock/Getty Images Plus; Westend61; Cahir Davitt/AWL Images; Ingolf Hatz/Cultura; Perboge/iStock Editorial/Getty Images Plus; Maremagnum/Photodisc; Ed Bock/Corbis; Jon Shireman/Photonica; Spaces Images/Blend Images; wakila/E+; ihoe/iStock/Getty Images Plus; kevinjeon00/E+; Vostok/Moment & Vostok/Moment; **U9**: Daft_Lion_Studio/iStock/Getty Images Plus; Zero Creatives/Cultura; GomezDavid/E+; Westend61; PeopleImages/E+; Don Mason/Blend Images; Ryan McVay/Photodisc; ewg3D/iStock/Getty Images Plus; jfoltyn/iStock/Getty Images Plus.

The following images are sourced from other libraries:
SU, U1, U3, U5, U8 & U9: Carboxylase/Shutterstock.

Illustration
Alex Herrerias: U1, U5, U6; Antonio Cuesta: SU, U3, U5, U6; Jose Rubio: U1, U4, U5.

Typesetting: Blooberry Design

Cover illustration: Collaborate Agency

Audio recordings: Creative Listening

Video production: Lucentum Digital

Freelance editing: Matthew Duffy, Nicola Foufouti, Jacqueline French